THIS IS THE BOOK THAT TAKES THE MYSTERY OUT OF INDIAN COOKING . . . BUT NOT THE MYSTIQUE!

❖ ❖ ❖

Most westerners enjoy Indian food—but fear its fiery side. Rest easy, restock your spice shelf and eat up: CURRIES WITHOUT WORRIES gives you a basic and practical understanding of Indian seasonings and cuisine. Easy recipes, sample menus and simple cooking techniques cover everything from appetizers to desserts. In no time at all you'll be serving such exciting and successfully prepared Indian dishes as:

- CHICKEN CURRY À LA MUSSOORIE—Stir-fried chicken in a sour cream sauce that melts in your mouth; the fragrant curry is topped with slivered almonds and fresh coriander
- EGGPLANT AND TOMATO CURRY—Garden-fresh baby eggplants and vine-ripened ruby red tomatoes simmered to perfection in a ginger-fennel-cayenne sauce
- KHICHDI or Real Kedgeree—Mung beans cooked with rice, meat, cinnamon sticks and cardamom pods; a nutritious and delicious meal-in-a-dish
- KULFI GALI WALI—Almonds, pistachios and crushed cardamom seeds flavor this smooth and golden ice cream; a centuries-old recipe!
- ROGHANJOSH—Lamb cooked in an aromatic gravy of cloves, onion, yoghurt, ginger and red pepper; an authentic Kashmiri specialty
- SAMOSA—Potatoes and peas or spiced ground meat fill this deep-fried spring roll; a favorite snack at tea time.

"Her culinary repertoire is put together in the best possible way . . . guaranteed to impress and a snap to make."

—*Indian Express*

CURRIES WITHOUT WORRIES

SUDHA KOUL

WARNER BOOKS

A Time Warner Company

Warner Books Edition
Copyright © 1983, 1989, 1993 by Sudha Koul
All rights reserved.
This Warner Books edition is published by arrangement with the author.
Warner Books, Inc., 1271 Avenue of the Americas, New York, NY 10020

Visit our Web site at http://warnerbooks.com

 A Time Warner Company

Printed in the United States of America
First Warner Books Printing: March 1996
10 9 8 7 6 5

Library of Congress Cataloging-in-Publication Data
Koul, Sudha.
    Curries without worries / Sudha Koul.—Warner Books ed.
        p.   cm.
    Originally published: Pennington, N.J. : Cashmir, c1989.
    Includes index.
    ISBN 0-446-67078-2 (trade pbk.)
    1. Cookery, India.   I. Title.
[TX724.5.I4K68   1996]
641.5954—dc20   95-8544
                                                                            CIP

Cover design by Julia Kushnirsky
Cover and text illustrations by David Montiel,
based on artwork by Sudha Koul
Book design by Giorgetta Bell McRee

For Shyamji

"Something is better than nothing."

Just a word . . .

I would never have written a cookbook if I had not come to live in the United States, and had no choice but to do the cooking myself. If my friends had not shown so much interest in the Indian meals I prepared for them, if my husband had not looked after the children while I typed upstairs, if Vinnie Ogra had not let me borrow her typewriter, if Agha Shahid Ali had not played Professor Higgins, I would not have ventured on this project. I certainly would never have completed it were it not for Charles Burt, connoisseur of Indian food and onetime resident of India, who told me that I should write this book and found the time amidst his various, more important tasks to guide me. It was his wife, my friend Betty, who gave me the necessary courage from day to day by applauding whatever snatches I read to her. And last but not least, I would like to thank Donna Brugman for all the time and help she gave me during the final preparations of this book.

All these things have come to pass and the book has been written. I hope it makes some contribution toward satisfying the growing curiosity of Americans about Indian cuisine. If it does, its purpose will have been served. The reader, particularly one with no prior experience in Indian cooking, will be well advised to go through the whole book before trying out the recipes. I hope that the informal, chatty style I have attempted will make the task relatively painless.

Sudha Koul

Pennington, 1983

This edition of *Curries Without Worries* would not have been possible without a great deal of help from Beth Huskamp, Kamla Koul, and Jeannine von Ballmoos.

Sudha Koul

Pennington, 1989

Contents

✳ ✳ ✳

CURRIES
WITHOUT
WORRIES

✳ ✳ ✳

Curries Without Worries— A Synopsis

Introduction: In this chapter I describe what an Indian meal consists of and how it is to be served. My intention is to show the reader that preparing an Indian meal is quite simple. Some common misconceptions are dealt with and rectified. There is a discussion on spices, utensils, and other important requisites for Indian cuisine. I also explain why and for whom the book was written.

Basic Recipes: Recipes for *garam masala, ghee,* and yoghurt to start you off!

Rice: I must confess that I was surprised to learn that most Americans consider preparing rice from scratch to be tricky. Keeping this in mind, I have given you detailed, easy-to-follow recipes and tips that should make every reader eager to cook rice. The recipes range from plain to lavish . . . all simple, and simply delicious!

Breads: Indian breads are unforgettable for one reason: there is nothing else like them. Usually made with wheat flour, they are utterly tasty. From among the staggering variety of Indian breads, I have chosen three of my favorite basic bread recipes.

Non-Vegetarian: Curries, roasts, kababs—they are all here and simplified beyond belief! Cuts and sizes of meats are specified, leaving as little as possible for the cook to figure out.

Vegetarian: There is an infinite number of ways to prepare vegetarian food on the Indian subcontinent. Making a selection was difficult. I settled on the most popular recipes. Hopefully, this will be an incentive to vegetarians to add to their growing repertoire of recipes.

Raita: A yoghurt-based vegetarian delight, *raita* is a natural food lover's dream-come-true. Always very popular with my friends here, it lends itself elegantly to innovation.

Salads, Chutneys, and a Pickle: For the adventurous, I have included simple recipes for Indian chutneys. Indian salads are quite unadventurous compared to their Western counterparts. They are meant to complement curries and to serve as a contrast to them. This they do superbly. My mother's Southern pickle recipe is thrown in as a bonus!

Desserts: Someone once described Indian sweets as confections ''concocted from milk that has simmered and thickened for a couple of months at least.'' This is a slight exaggeration! Most Indian sweets are made from *khoya*, which is a milk solid formed from simmering and thickening milk for a few hours! I hasten to add that the recipes here are dependable shortcuts to a sweet finale, requiring neither months nor even hours to prepare.

Snacks: So good you may want to serve them as entrees! However, they are usually served at tea time.

Menus: A list of possible combinations for a complete Indian meal is given at the end of the book.

Introduction

Most Americans seem to know what a Chinese, or Mexican, or Middle Eastern meal looks like. However, when it comes to Indian food, most people have a vague impression of an entree called curry, which contains mysterious ingredients and is too hot. Fortunately, this impression is changing. The number of Indians living in this country has grown tremendously, and there has been a great surge of interest in all things Indian. In fact so many Americans have fallen in love with Indian cuisine that some of the ingredients used in Indian cooking have become quite commonplace. Indian restaurants have blossomed everywhere and are patronized by an increasing number of Americans who ooh and aah over the food, and not because it is too hot! Naturally, fascination with the cuisine has led to a desire to cook Indian food at home.

I still remember the day when some very dear friends of my husband invited us for dinner and served an Indian meal. They had, on occasion, enjoyed Indian meals cooked by my husband and wanted to give his still quite new bride a surprise. And they did! I had come to the United States for the first time and was intrigued by the prospect of eating an Indian meal cooked by Americans. To my surprise they served a delectable looking vegetable curry and hot, fluffy rice . . . a simple and authentic Indian meal. I eagerly took a mouthful and bit into something hard and pungent, almost bitter. The quintessential Indian spice turmeric . . . in its natural state! Swallowing it rapidly, I thought to myself that the recipe must not have explained that ground turmeric was required. I cannot think of any spice used in Western cooking that would even approximate such a culinary disaster had it been added whole instead of ground.

Even a cookbook must be inspired, and this episode sowed the seeds of a desire to introduce my new friends to Indian cooking. I hope my relating this episode at the very beginning of the book will not make an apprehensive reader even more apprehensive. I must add that, after removing the remaining pieces of turmeric, I enjoyed a hearty and delicious meal. The food was not rich, heavy, overly spicy, or gourmet; rather, it consisted of wholesome, honest-to-goodness, everyday Indian preparations, thoroughly enjoyable and healthy, despite the aforementioned oversight. I was made to feel at home by the thoughtfulness that had gone into its preparation and by its superb quality.

A number of excellent books on gourmet Indian cooking are available in the United States. However, I find that the appetite for Indian food has overstepped the confines of gourmet clubs; people want to prepare the Indian equivalent of steak and potatoes or spaghetti and meatballs. Well, now you can do it, with this friendly little book for which you have been waiting!

I bought a Chinese wok a long time ago. With the wok came a little booklet containing a few recipes for Chinese preparations. This book has proven to be of greater use to me than some bulky Chinese cookbooks I own. Why? Because it is an uncomplicated introduction to Chinese cooking. It contains simple, but authentic and delicious, recipes which encourage you to try your hand at them. In my opinion, a lack of such an introduction to Indian cuisine is a justification for writing an Indian cookbook for beginners. The reader might still ask why one should bother with ordinary fare while preparing a meal intended to be exotic. The answer is that the flavors, appearance, indeed the whole experience, of an Indian meal—be it ever so simple—are in themselves exotic. Most people who try Indian food, even everyday fare, come back for more. Once you develop a taste for Indian food, you come to appreciate an entirely new culinary dimension. You cannot eat only gourmet dishes to fully appreciate the unique world of Indian cuisine.

It is not difficult . . .
the utensils are not elaborate . . .

At the risk of being barred from gourmet clubs, I must let you in on a secret. Most Indian dishes are simple and can be prepared in a short time. Cooking over open fires, as was the custom, hardly improves the flavor unless the recipe specifically calls for grilling. The pressure cooker is used often in Indian cooking now. I sense a disinclination to use the pressure cooker in this country. I shall consequently stick with pots and pans that pressurize neither the food nor the cook!

The best pots and pans for Indian cooking are heavy-bottomed, stainless steel saucepans or skillets. Non-stick pans are good for many things, but not for "browning" meats and vegetables, which is an integral aspect of Indian cooking. Stainless steel cooking spoons with long handles are best suited for Indian cooking.

For deep frying and for a host of other cooking procedures, Indians also use a type of wok called *kadhai*. The *kadhai* is heavier than most "oriental" woks and is superior for deep frying. This is because most Indian foods that are deep fried require the oil to be consistently very hot during the frying process, and hence, a heavy wok is preferable. However, if you do use the lighter wok, please regulate the heat.

Another Indian utensil indispensable for making breads is the *tawa* or flat, heavy griddle. A cast-iron pancake griddle is an excellent substitute.

For making Indian breads, it is a good idea to buy a one-piece rolling pin of smaller diameter than the common pastry rolling pin. Rolling pins meant for pastry consist of two pieces. This is not efficient for Indian breads which are rolled out much thinner than pastry. The best utensil is an Indian rolling pin, called a *belan*, which is perfectly suited for rolling out Indian breads. (See Figure 1, page 47.) You can find the *belan* in an Indian store.

"Curry" defined . . .

What is a basic Indian meal? As I mentioned earlier, the Indian equivalent of an everyday American meal would be hot rice and/or bread with steaming curry. To avoid confusion between hot (as in steaming hot) and hot (as in spicy hot), I shall call the former hot and the latter spicy.

This is a good place to bring up an old worry that most people have about Indian food—that it is too spicy. This is a myth that needs to be exposed! For a country that takes five alarm chili, jalapeño, hot Chinese mustard, or Japanese radish sauce in its stride, Indian food is a bowl of cherries! The comforting fact about Indian food is that its ingredients can almost always be altered to suit the palate. It is not like a soufflé that won't rise or a cake that won't bake. If you want to reduce the amount of spiciness in your cooking, you may do so. If, on the other hand, like a colleague of my husband, you don't feel you have had Indian food until you've used up all the tissue paper in the house, that is your privilege, and you may add pepper to your taste. *No* recipe in this book is for a lethally spicy dish.

This brings us to THE QUESTION: what is a curry? I must mention here a discovery I made recently. There are some people who think that curry is a spice that grows on plants, like peppers or cardamoms. Consequently, they say that they like to cook their food with curry. That is like saying you like to cook with soufflés. A curry is a stewlike preparation of meats and/or vegetables, which is eaten with hot rice and/or bread. It is similar to meatballs in sauce on spaghetti. However, please note that if curry is served with breads, it is not placed on top of the bread; rather, it is served on the side.

The curry may be very dry or may have a lot of gravy. Some people use the word "sauce," but I think "gravy" is a better word since it is formed from the juice of the meat or vegetable. A sauce is prepared separately, and lacks the essence of the meat or vegetable. A good rule of thumb is that curries eaten with breads have a thickish gravy and those eaten with rice have a gravy that is a bit thinner. Remember also that vegetables taste better with a thicker gravy, whereas meat and poultry make rich juices that permit thinner gravies.

Meats usually give out some moisture when they are cooked slowly. This results in the gravy being a bit thinner than I like it to be. To remedy this, I simmer the curry uncovered until I achieve the thickness I want. You can do the same.

The driest form of meat preparation is the *tandoori*, or roast, style. The meat is marinated in spices and yoghurt, but the marinade is almost completely absorbed during the cooking process. However, Indian curries must always be eaten with rice or bread. Even *tandoori* entrees are served with some form of bread, usually a yeast bread called *nan*.

In some parts of India, breads called *chappati* or *roti* or *phulki* are more popular than rice. In fact, they form the staple. However, in most regions of the country, whether breads are served or not, rice is almost always served. Rice may be cooked plain or as a *pullao* (pilaf), with vegetables and/or meat. Similarly, breads may be simple or elaborate.

So far we have three items on our menu: curry, rice, and bread. The fourth, and equally indispensable, item is *dal*, or lentils. *Dal* is the major source of protein in India, particularly for vegetarians. A *dal* does not look very different from lentil soup, although the cooking process is different. In any case, a well-cooked *dal* is delicious enough to make you forget about animal protein! Supermarket lentils work well in most *dal* recipes. However, if a recipe requires a specific *dal*, you may have to buy it at an Indian grocery or a natural food store.

Accoutrements . . .

A must at an Indian meal is yoghurt. It is believed to have all kinds of medicinal and therapeutic properties. It cools in the summer, calms upset stomachs, and, in general, contributes to longevity. Yoghurt is usually eaten plain, but sometimes broiled, boiled, chopped, or grated vegetables or fruit are added, and the concoction is called *raita*. I find that this is a particular favorite with my American friends. This is also a preparation with which an imaginative cook can innovate in infinite ways.

In Indian cooking yoghurt always means plain yoghurt. Even a yoghurt mildly flavored with vanilla is "out."

Invariably, an Indian meal includes a salad of some kind. Those who cannot afford a fancy salad have a chopped onion and/or a hot green pepper along with their meal. In middle-class homes, a salad (pronounced *salaad*) usually consists of very finely chopped or sliced vegetables tossed together and sprinkled with salt, pepper, and fresh lime juice or vinegar. Only a few vegetables are used for salads, and the attitude toward experimentation is rather conservative.

Finally, we come to the condiments, or little palate teasers, which for some people are an indispensable part of an Indian meal. These are *papads* or *pappadoms*, chutneys, and pickles.

Papads are a lentil-based, tortilla-like cracker which can be crumbled into rice and curry, or nibbled before dinner as an appetizer. The preparation of *papads* is better left to the commercial manufacturers and certainly does not need to be included in a beginner's cookbook. Any Indian store stocks a good variety of *papads*.

Chutneys have been immortalized in the Western world, particularly in the United Kingdom, by Major Grey, and quite a good selection is available here. However, what often passes for chutney belongs more to the realm of preserves. Fresh chutneys, more common in India, are quite different from preserves in texture and taste. Preserves are usually sweet and, more often than not, made with lime or mangoes. However, fresh chutneys may be made of mouth-watering combinations of mint, coriander, dates, tomatoes, peppers, walnuts, coconut, or sour cherries. Chutneys are incredibly easy to prepare, and I have included a few recipes.

Indian pickles, called *achar*, are usually based in mustard oil and are very spicy, very tangy. They may take some getting used to! Every region has its folklore about which area makes the deadliest pickles. Some pickles are allegedly so spicy and peppery that one spoonful burns right through the rice to the plate. One hesitates to think of what it might do to one's alimentary canal. Food for thought?

The fact remains that making Indian pickles at home is a bit complicated. Fortunately, pickles lend themselves very nicely to bottling and Indian stores stock excellent pickles of the highest quality. I have given you a simple recipe for one of my favorite pickles. This pickle is not available in stores.

Sweetmeats, called *mithai* in India, are often served at high tea or at festive occasions. However, at an Indian meal, you may or may not be served dessert. It depends upon where you are in India. When dessert *is* served, it is traditionally an Indian equivalent of a rice pudding, called *khir* or *payasam* or *firuine*. Since most Americans find a meal without a dessert to be incomplete, I have included a few choice recipes for *mithai*.

Curry explained . . .

So there you have it; the mystery of what makes up a typical Indian meal is unraveled! A few further explanations are in order. The fare served to the Moghul emperors of India was, no doubt, far more intricately designed and served than are the meals at my mother's house in India. However, rich food, even if it is *moghlai*, is not something you can have every day without considerable damage to your well-being. "*Moghlai*" cuisine is now the speciality of restaurants and is far richer than everyday Indian cooking, although the latter is influenced by the former. Besides, as I have mentioned earlier, quite a few excellent books have been written on gourmet Indian cuisine. It is the wonderful range of delicious and light everyday Indian cookery that has been neglected. This book seeks to fill that void.

I often recall the story my American sister-in-law told me about the first time she had an Indian meal. At the time, she had no idea that she would one day marry an Indian. She had gone to Toronto with friends who loved Indian food. They could not persuade her to try it. Finally, they decided that she should wait for them to eat, and she would eat later at another restaurant. While waiting for them to finish their meal, she nibbled at a piece of *tandoori* chicken, and the rest, so to speak, is history. I will not let Indian cookery take the credit for her later decisions in life, but I will certainly say it was a case of coming to scoff and remaining to pray. They left the restaurant much later than planned. This kind of conversion is more the rule than the exception, and it is for friends like her that I am writing this book.

Curry universal . . .

One more diversion before we get on with the recipes. There is no national Indian cuisine. Just as Chinese cuisine varies from province to province, so does Indian cooking. Since I am from the north of India, my recipes are a bit biased in that direction. However, most of the recipes in this book are those that have gained popularity all over India. These are also the dishes most familiar to Americans who frequent Indian restaurants.

I have stayed away from dishes that require the technical expertise of those who can whirl pizza dough into the sky and successfully retrieve it. In short, I have introduced you to the kind of fare you would have at my mother's house and at the houses of my friends all over India. This book contains tested and tried recipes from relatives and friends, and their names go with the recipes. I have made some modifications in order to further simplify procedures.

The ingredients . . .
readily available

The other day, in a bookstore, I overheard a lady talking to the salesclerk. She had just bought a gigantic book on Asian cookery and was complaining that the bigger task was yet at hand—procuring spices and utensils. Indeed, when you look at an Indian cookbook for the first time, it may look as though every recipe is complicated, because it calls for so many ingredients. The fact is, that once you have a "starter kit" of spices, you will use the same ingredients again and again in different combinations. I remember that when I came to the United States, I had to go out and stock up on oregano, Parmesan, rosemary, thyme, parsley, tarragon, black pepper, white pepper, Worcestershire sauce, basil, sage, chives, spaghetti, tartar sauce, baking soda, baking powder . . . I could go on and on. Indian cooking *is* a different cuisine, but once you have obtained the basic spices and utensils I have described, you are set to explore a wonderful new subcontinent of food! It may come as a surprise to you that the crucial spices for most Indian dishes can all be found in the average supermarket, sometimes in the gourmet section.

There are a few spices used in Indian cooking which are not yet readily available in American supermarkets, such as asafoetida (called *hing* in India). Even minute quantities of this resin-like substance produce a unique aroma. However, when I moved to our new house in New Jersey, I was miles away from an Indian grocery, and I did very well without *hing*. In fact, no one noticed its absence. I can see a lot of fanatical eyebrows go up at that sentence! If you insist, you can buy it at the local Indian store. I assure you that *hing* is not to Indian food what dough is to pizza.

Tamarind, another important ingredient, particularly for south Indian cooking, is readily available only in the Indian groceries. It is the sour pulp of the fruit of the tamarind tree and when added to a preparation it imparts to it a tart flavor, brownish coloring, and something appetizingly undefinable.

Now we come to the question that you have so patiently waited to ask. What about curry powder? This is one thing almost everybody knows about. When curry powder is added to fricasseed chicken, for example, the chicken is, by common consent, converted to curry. By inference, anything with a dash of curry powder qualifies it as a curry. Not so! Indians do not use curry powder as it is known in the West. Using a single combination of *masalas* (spices) for all curries is unheard of. It is as unthinkable as using the same herbs for all Western dishes. Most Indian homes use a blend of spices, called *garam masala*, for a final garnish. I have given you a recipe for *garam masala*, which is also excellent for *tandoori* meats. Of late, pre-mixed spices for different dishes have become available even in India (a boon for working women)! Convenience is probably one explanation for the origin of curry powder. Some packaged varieties of pre-mixed spices are available in the Indian grocery stores or gourmet sections of some supermarkets here.

Seasonings I use fresh are:

Coriander
Curry leaf (similar to bay leaf; just adding curry leaf does not make a curry)
Garlic
Fresh ginger
Hot green peppers or "chillies"
Mint

Onions
Scallions

In orthodox Indian households dry *masalas* are ground freshly every day. However, in the homes of those of us who have no desire to spend most of our lives in the kitchen or to hire someone just to pulverize spices, dry spices, whole and ground, can be bottled and stored in separate jars.

The dry seasonings on my shelves are:

Asafoetida (*hing*) . . . . powdered or in small lumps
Bay leaves . . . . whole
Black pepper . . . . whole and ground
Black cardamom (*badi illachi*) . . . . whole, crushed, or ground
Black cumin seeds . . . . whole
Cardamom . . . . pods or seeds; whole, crushed, or ground
Cayenne pepper . . . . ground
Cinnamon . . . . whole, crushed, or ground
Cloves . . . . whole or ground
Coriander seeds . . . . crushed or ground
Curry leaves . . . . whole
Cumin seeds . . . . whole or ground
Dry hot red peppers . . . . crushed or whole
Fennel seeds . . . . whole or ground
Fenugreek seeds . . . . whole or ground
Ginger . . . . ground to a powder
Mustard seeds . . . . whole, sometimes ground
Nutmeg . . . . grated or ground
Onion seeds . . . . whole
Turmeric . . . . ground

Note: Turmeric is beneficial to your system, but its stains are difficult to remove. So, be careful while using it.

I hesitate to include saffron in either herbs or spices, since it is quite delicate, extraordinary, and in a class by itself. Perhaps, being a native of Kashmir, which has the most spectacular saffron fields in the world, I have a special feeling for saffron.

I also have a great partiality for fresh coriander, called *dhania* in India. It looks like parsley, but the similarity ends there. It adds a fantastic dimension of flavor and fragrance to Indian food. It is also used in Italian, Armenian, Mexican, and Chinese cooking. In the last couple of years I have been able to find it quite easily in the supermarkets here. It is wonderful to see these changes. I grow mine in the summer, by soaking a handful of coriander seeds in a cup of water overnight and sowing them the next day. It takes about a couple of months to become identifiable as coriander, but it is worth the wait to me!

So, this is the assortment I have on my kitchen shelves, and it comes, almost entirely, from supermarkets. I will not dispute the fact that this is not a complete list of Indian spices and herbs, but it will suffice for most people who cook Indian food. At any rate, I have managed fairly well with this list and have found my way to my husband's heart and to the hearts of some friends. They have never questioned the authenticity of my preparations!

You can be assured that all the recipes in this book are truly Indian. The only exception, I must confess, is the Mango Soufflé which I have included here because it is simple, unusual, and delicious.

This book is an attempt at helping West meet East. The meeting place is not in the recipe, which is purely Indian, but in the enjoyment of the cuisine.

The cooking medium . . .

In India, mustard seed oil, coconut oil, sesame seed oil, peanut oil, etc., are used in different regions. I find corn oil a perfect (also healthy) substitute for all of these, since it does not have an intrusive flavor.

Clarified, strained butter, or *ghee*, is also used in India. Regular butter works just as well, but if you do use butter instead of *ghee*, melt it first on low heat before you heat it up for the recipe. Otherwise it might burn. If you want to use *ghee*, which has a richer flavor than butter, you can make it at home. The method is simple and is given in the basic recipe section. For the sake of convenience, I shall use the word *ghee* in the recipes unless butter is specifically called for.

A final word on ingredients . . .

Be sure to have a supply of dry nuts such as almonds, walnuts, pistachios, and cashews, as these are used in many special dishes.

Curry served . . .

How is an Indian meal to be served? The traditional method is to serve food on a *thali*, or large metal plate of either silver, brass, or stainless steel. The rice is placed in a little heap at the center, and the dishes are served in very small bowls (or *katoris*) set around the rice. Very rarely is a meal served course by course. In modern households, *thalis* and *katoris* have been replaced with smaller china or stainless steel plates. The serving dishes are placed at the center of the table, as they are here, and passed around for people to help themselves.

I can anticipate the next questions. How do you help yourself? What comes first? The usual procedure is to take a small helping of rice or bread in the center of your plate and then to place the various entrees and accompaniments around it. If you prefer, you may take a small serving of rice with one entree, then a second serving of rice with another entree, and so on. Or, you may eat rice or bread with all the entrees. There are no hard and fast rules. Small bowls for *dals* or curries with a lot of gravy are very good substitutes for the *katoris* used in India. Your guests can place their bowls on the sides of their plates, and help themselves with a teaspoon.

Vegetarians should be particularly delighted to see how balanced, nutritious, and delicious an Indian vegetarian meal is. The variety of vegetarian dishes from India is practically infinite. I should point out that if vegetables done Indian-style appear over-cooked, it is because Indians are wary of undercooking their vegetables. You can also improvise and cook vegetables to the degree of tenderness you prefer.

Another thing to keep in mind is that "vegetarian" in India means the total absence of meat, fish, chicken, egg, or the stock or flavoring thereof. This is due to personal or religious reasons. Our family is non-vegetarian, and sometimes I add stock or bouillon to vegetarian recipes instead of water. Of course this is only when I am not entertaining vegetarian friends. It seems to add a little something to the flavor, but that may just be the prejudiced view of an avid non-vegetarian!

I have given you a list of possible menus for Indian meals at the end of the book. There are no stringent rules for determining combinations, only those dictated by taste.

When shopping . . .

Always buy fresh lamb. If your local supermarkets do not have a good selection of fresh lamb, try a farmer's market. When you buy lamb and have it ground, it is a good idea to ask the butcher to trim all the fat before grinding it. Ground turkey is readily available now, and it is being touted as the healthiest form of ground meat. I use it almost all the time and find it a lean and healthy substitute for ground lamb without any of the flavor one normally associates with turkey. In fact, it is so lean that I sometimes add a spoonful of corn oil to it. In any event, unless I inform my guests, they always assume they are eating either ground beef or lamb. It's quite amazing.

Indians do not, by and large, eat beef. However, most Americans prefer beef to lamb, and you may substitute beef for the lamb recipes. Quite a few Indians here do that, and they tell me that if the cut of beef is lean and tender, there is hardly any noticeable difference in taste.

When shopping for chicken, try to buy the smallest variety, fryers or Cornish game hens. The smaller the chicken, the better suited it is to Indian cooking. This could be due to the fact that large birds cannot absorb the spices as well as the smaller birds can.

A greater variety of fish is available in India; brook trout in the north in Kashmir, river and lake fish in the mainland, and a plentitude of seafood in the vast coastal areas to the south.

For the recipes I have given you, a mild, white-fleshed fish such as flounder, catfish, halibut, orange roughy, cod, or sole is the best choice.

Although frozen peas are indispensable, in general, the results are much better when you use fresh vegetables.

IMPORTANT: HAVE ALL YOUR INGREDIENTS READY BEFORE YOU COOK. IF YOU HAVE OIL HEATING ON THE BURNER, THERE MAY NOT BE ENOUGH TIME TO GO LOOKING FOR CUMIN SEEDS, OR TO START CHOPPING ONIONS!

Let's try some recipes now!

Just a minute . . .

I have had a busy post office box since my book was published, and received many helpful and interesting queries. I decided to share my replies with all of you!

Add or reduce spices to taste. Try a recipe to decide how spicy you want it. I have attempted the impossible, trying to strike at that optimal level of spiciness that appeals to everyone! (see page 9). If you find you like a particular spice, add a little more. No cardinal rule will be violated by improvising. Cuisines evolve and I am pretty certain that those that adapt the best survive. Does a cup of chopped coriander mean loosely or tightly packed? The answer is how much do you like coriander? Yes, cilantro is the same as coriander. If you double a recipe, reduce some of the stronger spices. You should not double everything. Be prepared for some trial and error. Turmeric can only replace the color of saffron, never its flavor.

For reasons of health or taste, you may substitute oil or vegetable shortening for *ghee* and reduce the amount you use. You can use non-fat or low-fat yoghurt instead of whole milk yoghurt. The dish will not be as creamy, but then that, perhaps, is what you want. Thus, some prefer brown or wild rice to long grained or *basmati*. Naturally, it tastes different. All I say is, enjoy yourself! A rice cooker is fine for cooking plain rice.

Do not panic if foam appears on top of boiling *dal*. If you have washed your *dal*, this is not scum or dirt! Skim off the foam, or wait for it to settle down, which it should do after you have added salt.

You may prepare entrees ahead of time, except when the recipe specifically calls for the dish to be served immediately. Some people believe that most Indian dishes taste better the next day as the spices have had time to blend well into the other ingredients. Naturally, you must refrigerate the dish if you do not plan to serve it the same day.

Remember, this is not a book for fanatics. It is an authentic Indian cookbook used by genuine cooks of Indian cuisine. Adjustments have been made to a new time and place. No cuisine stipulates only one way of making a dish. Betty's apple pie tastes different from Pam's; both are real and delicious. You may not be able to replicate that *dal* you had at a friend's house, but there are as many ways to cook *dal* as there are friends! I have selected the best recipes I came across.

I wish you many curries and no worries!

Basic
Recipes

Garam Masala

1 large cinnamon stick, or 2 medium sticks, coarsely crushed
1 tablespoon whole cumin seeds
1 tablespoon coriander seeds
1 tablespoon peppercorns
1 tablespoon cardamom seeds
1 tablespoon cloves
1 tablespoon fennel seeds
½ teaspoon grated nutmeg

Preheat the oven to 350°F. for 10 minutes. Spread out all the spices, from cinnamon to nutmeg, in a single layer on a cookie sheet. Place the cookie sheet in the oven for 20 minutes until the aroma of toasted spices begins to emanate. Remove from oven, and cool completely at room temperature. Then, grind spices together in a blender until all the spices are reduced to a powder. The cinnamon may be a little coarse, but you can sift the spices and grind the coarse pieces again. This yields about ½ cup. You can store the *masala* in a tightly capped bottle for future use. It should keep for several months. This book has many recipes that require this *masala*. If you plan to make these recipes often, it is a good idea to double or triple the amount of *masala* you make and store it.

Ghee

Melt and simmer a pound of unsalted butter in a very heavy saucepan at the lowest possible heat until a clear, yellowish liquid forms on top and almost all the sediment from the butter has settled at the bottom. This should take about 15 minutes. Cool to room temperature. Strain, and pour into a jar that can be covered tightly. Any foam still floating at the top can be removed by straining. The main point is that when a clear, yellowish liquid has formed from the butter, and some sediment has settled at the bottom, the *ghee* is ready. Any further simmering may cause the *ghee* to burn and turn into a brown liquid, which is not what you want. The *ghee* should keep for many months.

Yoghurt

1 quart whole milk
2 tablespoons plain yoghurt

1. Bring the milk to a boil in a 6-quart saucepan. Stir to prevent overflow when the milk starts to boil. When milk starts to boil, lower heat to lowest point possible, and simmer for 10 minutes.

2. Allow milk to cool for about half an hour. It should be very warm when you put your finger in to test it, but not so hot that you cannot put your finger into it comfortably.

3. Next, mix the yoghurt with 2 tablespoons of the milk and mix well into the rest of the milk.

4. Cover with a lid and wrap in a very thick towel or cloth. Keep undisturbed in a draft-free place overnight.

5. Remember:
- Once you place the yoghurt to set, do not disturb!
- If the yoghurt turns out watery or sour it means the milk was too hot when you mixed in the culture.
- If the yoghurt does not form, the milk was not warm enough or the culture was too mild.
- Yoghurt takes less time to form in warm weather.

6. The way to check whether it has formed is to lift the lid and blow on it. If it has not set, cover and keep for a few more hours undisturbed.

Rice

There are two basic ways to cook rice.

1. Plain, i.e., boiled with water

2. Cooked with other ingredients

When other ingredients are added to rice, it may be cooked as a *biryani*, *pullao*, or *khichdi*. I have given you basic recipes for these variations. These dishes are quite rich and can be eaten with only a *raita* or a salad as an accompaniment. However, other entrees can be included for grander feasts.

Keep in mind:

1. Regular long grained rice takes a little longer to cook than *basmati* rice.

2. Stir the rice only before the grains have become tender, or else the grains will break and the rice will become lumpy.

Plain Boiled Rice

6 cups water
1 cup long grained rice

1. Bring water to a boil on high heat in a 4-quart saucepan. Add the rice, stirring constantly. Lower the heat to medium and cook for 15 minutes, stirring once or twice to prevent the rice from sticking to the bottom of the pan. When the rice starts puffing up, drain off the water in a soup strainer. Transfer the rice back to the saucepan, lower the heat to the lowest point, and cover the saucepan. Cook for 5 minutes. Serve hot. It is safer to cook rice with less water. If you use too much to start with, there is no way out. However, if after following the instructions above, the rice is not tender enough, add 3 tablespoons of water, cover, and continue to cook on the lowest possible heat for another 5 minutes. Add the water by pouring it over the rice, as you pour syrup over pancakes. Do not stir.

2. Leftover rice is best reheated by steaming.

If you prefer to cook the rice without draining off the water, this is the method:

1 cup rice
2 cups water

1. Bring the rice and water to a boil on high heat and continue to boil for 2 minutes, stirring off and on to prevent the rice from sticking to the bottom of the pan. Reduce heat to the lowest point, cover, and cook for about 15 minutes, until the rice is puffy and tender. If the rice appears a little hard after following the above procedure, pour 3 tablespoons of water over it, cover, and cook on the lowest heat for another 5 minutes.

2. Serve hot.

Serves 2

Vegetable *Pullao*

4 tablespoons *ghee* **(page 24)**
1 medium onion, chopped
1 teaspoon very finely chopped fresh ginger
½ teaspoon ground turmeric
3 cloves
2 small cinnamon sticks
2 bay leaves
2 cardamom pods, coarsely crushed
½ teaspoon whole cumin seeds
½ cup frozen peas
1½ cups cubed or chopped vegetables, i.e., potatoes, cauliflower florets (fresh or frozen). You may use other vegetables of your choice, provided they are cut into small pieces and are of the crunchy variety. Squash, pumpkins, or leafy vegetables should not be used in a *pullao.*
1 cup long grained rice, preferably *basmati*
2½ cups water. If this is not a vegetarian vegetable *pullao,* **you could substitute stock or bouillon for the water. This is to be added in place of the water, not in addition to it.**
Salt to taste
A pinch of saffron, soaked in 5 tablespoons of water

1. Heat the *ghee* in a 4-quart saucepan on high heat for 1 minute. Add the onion, ginger, and turmeric, and fry for 1 minute. Add the cloves, cinnamon, bay leaves, cardamom pods, and cumin seeds. Stir well to prevent burning and sticking to the pan. Fry for a few seconds. Add the vegetables, and stir fry for 2 minutes. Add the rice, and stir briskly for a few seconds. Add the water (or stock) and salt, stirring constantly. When the entire contents of the saucepan begin to boil, reduce heat to the lowest possible point, add saffron with the water, stir, and cover. Cook for 15 minutes.

2. The vegetables may rise to the top, but do not stir after the rice has started boiling, as this will cause the rice to break and become lumpy.

3. Serve hot.

Serves 4

Nana's Lamb *Biryani*

Lamb, rice, tomatoes, and saffron in a rich biryani

8 tablespoons *ghee* (page 24)
3 large onions, chopped
2 tablespoons chopped fresh ginger
2 cloves garlic, minced
2 pounds lean fresh leg of lamb, cut into approximately 2″ × 2″ × 1″ pieces
1 teaspoon ground cayenne pepper
½ cup plain, whole milk yoghurt
2 medium tomatoes, finely chopped
4 cardamom pods, crushed
2 cinnamon sticks
8 cloves
3 bay leaves
Salt to taste
8 cups water
2 cups long grained rice, preferably *basmati*
Peels from 2 quartered oranges
12 bay leaves
½ cup blanched peeled raw almonds
A good pinch of saffron, soaked for an hour in ½ cup water
2 tablespoons butter, cut into small cubes

1. Heat the *ghee* in a 6-quart saucepan on high heat. Add the onions, ginger, and garlic, and stir fry until reddish. Add the lamb, and stir fry till it turns a golden brown. Take care that the lamb does not stick to the pan and burn. Stir occasionally to prevent this. However, stirring too often prevents the lamb from browning. This part requires the utmost attention of the cook.

2. When the lamb is nicely browned, reduce the heat to medium high.

3. Add the cayenne pepper, yoghurt, tomatoes, cardamom, cinnamon, and cloves; fry for a couple of minutes. Add the bay leaves and salt; bring to a boil. Cover, reduce heat to low, and cook for half an hour. Set aside.

4. In a separate saucepan, bring 8 cups of water to a boil. Add the rice, stir, and continue to boil on medium high heat for 5 minutes. Drain off all the water in a soup strainer. Set rice aside.

5. Line the bottom of a 4-quart saucepan with the orange peels (inside up) and the bay leaves. Spoon a layer of rice on the peels and bay leaves, enough to cover them. Next, add a layer of the cooked meat without the gravy, using a slotted spoon. Now, spoon another layer of rice on the meat, and repeat until you have layered all the rice and meat. The top layer should be rice. Spoon the gravy (from the meat) in a circle on the edge of the rice. Scatter the almonds on top, in the center. Pour the saffron with the water inside the ring of gravy. Now, if the *biryani* is seen from the top, it should have almonds in the middle, a ring of saffron around the almonds, and a ring of gravy around the saffron. Dot the top with the butter cubes. Cover the saucepan, and cook the *biryani* on the stove top on the lowest heat for about half an hour.

6. Serve hot.

Serves 6

Note: When you serve the *biryani*, remove the orange peels and bay leaves.

Mom's Popular Lamb *Pullao* from Kashmir

2 pounds lean sliced shoulder of lamb, each slice divided into 2 pieces
3 cups water
1 teaspoon ground turmeric
½ teaspoon ginger powder
1 teaspoon ground fennel seeds
5 cloves
Salt to taste
6 tablespoons *ghee* (page 24)
6 bay leaves
1 cup long grained rice
A good pinch of saffron
3 tablespoons plain, whole milk yoghurt
3 cardamom pods, crushed
½ teaspoon ground cumin seeds
1 cinnamon stick
1 cup sliced onions
3 tablespoons oil
¾ cup raw almonds and/or cashews
3 hard boiled eggs, sliced

1. Place the meat in a 6-quart saucepan. Add the water, turmeric, ginger, fennel, cloves, and salt. Bring to a boil, reduce heat to low, cover, and cook for half an hour. With a slotted spoon, remove the meat from the gravy, and set aside. Measure and set aside the gravy.

2. Heat the *ghee* on high heat in a 6-quart saucepan. Add the meat and bay leaves, and fry until the meat is crisp and golden brown. Reduce heat to medium.

3. Add the rice to the meat. Stir fry briskly, until the rice is well fried. This should take a few seconds.

4. You will need about 2½ cups of liquid for the rice to cook. If the gravy from the meat is 2½ cups, add it to the rice. If it is less, add water to make 2½ cups. In either case, use only 2½ cups.

5. Stir. Add the saffron, yoghurt, cardamom, cumin, and cinnamon; stir well. Bring to a boil. Cover, reduce heat to the lowest point, and cook until the rice is tender and puffy. This should take 15 to 20 minutes.

6. Fry the onions in oil on medium high heat until reddish and crisp. Remove with slotted spoon. Set aside.

7. Fry the nuts until golden. Remove with slotted spoon. Set aside.

8. When ready to serve, spoon *pullao* onto an oval platter. Scatter the onions on top, and edge the platter with the fried nuts and sliced eggs.

9. Serve hot.

Serves 4

Khichdi with Moong and Meat, or Real Kedgeree

Americans are familiar with moong beans, the source of bean sprouts. Whole or split, moong beans are a perennial favorite in India and are used in innumerable dishes. Here moong is cooked with rice and meat to form a nutritious and delicious meal-in-one!

1 cup moong beans soaked for 6 hours in 4 cups of water
6 tablespoons *ghee* (page 24)
1 teaspoon whole cumin seeds
5 cloves
2 pounds very lean lamb, cut into 2-inch cubes
1 teaspoon ground turmeric
Salt to taste
4 cardamom pods, lightly crushed
2 cinnamon sticks
3 bay leaves
½ teaspoon ginger powder
2 teaspoons ground fennel seeds
3 cups water
2 cups long grained rice

1. Drain and reserve the water from the moong beans. Set the moong aside.

2. Heat the *ghee* on medium high heat in a 6-quart saucepan. Add the cumin seeds, and stir until they sizzle. Add the cloves and meat.

3. Brown meat well.

4. Add the turmeric, salt, cardamom, cinnamon, bay leaves, ginger powder, and fennel. Stir briskly to fry all the spices and meat together for a few seconds.

5. Add 3 cups of water and the water from the beans to the meat. Stir, and bring to a boil. Reduce the heat to low, cover, and cook for 20 minutes.

6. Remove from heat.

7. Drain and measure the gravy from the meat, and set it aside.

8. Return meat to stove top.

9. Add the rice and the moong to the meat. Stir fry on high heat for a few seconds. Next, add 4 cups of the gravy. (If there is not enough gravy, add water to it to make 4 cups of liquid.)

10. Stir, bring to a boil, cover, lower heat to lowest point, and cook this way for about 15 minutes or until the rice is done.

11. Serve hot.

Serves 6

Breads

CHAPPATI: An everyday bread, also called *roti* or *phulki*, a *chappati* is rolled out round and flat, like a tortilla. Traditionally, it is toasted on a griddle and inflated on an open fire. The method given here is a simplified one, although the results are equally good.

PURI: Made with whole wheat flour and a little oil, a *puri* is rolled out flat and round and then deep fried. It should ideally puff up into a translucent, round shape when fried.

PARATHA: A layered bread, *paratha* is folded and rolled out flat into round, square, or triangular shapes. Made with whole wheat flour and either butter, or *ghee*, or shortening, *parathas* can be cooked like *chappatis* or fried like pancakes. And this is not all! One can make them plain or stuff them with vegetables or meat.

The *chappati* is the thinnest bread. The *puri* is thicker, and the *paratha* is the thickest, particularly the stuffed type.

These are all non-yeast, everyday breads. It is, frankly, difficult to make very fine *chappatis* with the whole wheat flour that is available in most supermarkets. I feel that mixing whole wheat flour with all purpose flour, in half and half proportions, makes a very nice dough for all these recipes. If you are a devotee of whole wheat and will not brook any mixture, that is fine too. The breads are going to be a bit coarse, but will still be delicious. If you are a devotee of the authentic, then your local Indian grocery (and sometimes the Chinese) is a good source for *chappati* flour made from whole wheat. However, for the sake of convenience I shall refer to the flour used as whole wheat flour, and leave the choice of what you use to you. All purpose white flour is not recommended.

All Indian breads are eaten hot off the griddle. You can make them ahead of time and keep them warm or reheat them in the oven. This is a good place to make the point that kept coming to mind while I was trying and testing the recipes for this book. It is amazing how heat levels differ in both cooking ranges and griddles. The main thing to remember while making the breads is that the griddle should not be so hot that the bread gives off a burning smell the second you start to cook it. It is far better for the heat to be a little low than too high. This is because the breads cook in a matter of seconds, or a couple of minutes, at the most. The other thing to keep in mind is that sometimes even the most seasoned (and regular) cook of Indian food has to sacrifice the first *chappati* or *puri* or *paratha* to test the waters. You have to get an idea of how hot the griddle or the cooking range is, and one *chappati* or *puri* or *paratha* is a small price to pay.

Chappatis, as taught by Pichi

½ cup cold water*
1 cup whole wheat flour
A small bowl of extra flour for patting down and rolling out the *chappatis*

1. Add the water to the flour, a little at a time, and mix well. Knead well until a soft, but not sticky or wet, dough is made. This should take a few minutes. (If you are using a food processor, follow the instructions to make dough.) The dough should tear easily when you pull a piece off. Cover with a damp cloth, and let it rest for an hour prior to cooking. This improves the consistency of the dough. When you are ready to make the *chappatis*, roll the dough into a "log," approximately the shape of commercially prepared frozen cookie dough. Cut into 10 portions as you would for cookies (Figure 2, page 47). Roll each portion into a ball, using the palms of your hands and moving them in a circular motion as you would if you were applying lotion to your palms.

*You may need a teaspoon or two more, or less, than ½ cup of water. This is because, like cooking ranges, cup sizes differ, and in such small amounts that little difference can make a big difference!

2. Place the ball in the extra flour; press it down in the center with three fingers, first on one side, then on the other. Now it will look like a patty.

3. Next, on a flat surface, roll out a *chappati* to about the same thickness as a tortilla and about 4½ inches in diameter. If you roll it out much more than that, it may not inflate well.

4. The art of rolling out a *chappati* is to be mastered. If your first *chappati* bears a striking resemblance to the map of the United States, do not be disheartened. You may be surprised to see how near perfect your next *chappati* will be.

5. One way of rolling out the *chappati* is to first roll out a slightly elongated piece, then turn it around, so that the narrow side is rolled out, making it round. You can repeat this process until the *chappati* is roundish and has a diameter of about 4½ inches. The *chappati* has to be rolled out a little at a time. If you roll out one side too long, you may tear the *chappati* and will then have to roll it into a ball and start all over again.

6. You may add a little flour to facilitate the rolling. I find that, compared to other flours, all purpose flour makes rolling out very easy. (You should dust off the extra flour by blowing on the *chappati* before you place it on the griddle.) Acquiring an Indian rolling pin, as stated earlier, will make the task of rolling out *chappatis* much easier. Applying a gentle pressure, roll out the *chappati* in a backward and forward motion, till you have a nice round shape. If I could learn to do it, you certainly can!

7. Roll out all the *chappatis* at the same time so that you can cook them one after the other, instead of having to stop and roll them out one at a time.

8. Cover the rolled out *chappatis* with a damp, muslin type of cloth to prevent them from drying out before cooking. The important thing is that you spread them out on a counter or tray: *Do not place them on top of each other.* Otherwise, you might find that they have turned into a solid mass. I had this nightmarish experience once, and never fail to pass this tip on to my friends.

9. If, on the other hand, you plan to roll out the *chappatis* one at a time, cover the dough with a light, damp cloth while you do the toasting.

10. When you are all set to cook the *chappatis*, heat a pancake griddle, or *tawa*, on medium heat for at least 10 minutes. Reduce the heat to low. It was difficult to agree upon exact times and temperatures for breads that are cooked in a jiffy, but I have tried to be as exact as I possibly could. The important thing to remember is that it is better to have the heat low than high. A little experience is the best guide in this matter.

11. When you think the griddle is right to toast the *chappati* gently, place the *chappati* in the center of the griddle.

12. After half a minute, when the *chappati* changes color all over, lift with a spatula and turn over. Toast the bread on the other side for half a minute. Turn over. With a small hand towel (folded twice), gently press the edges of the *chappati* down. It will start inflating. Then very gently, press the center down so that the *chappati* inflates into a roundish, puffed bread. This should take about a minute. Now the *chappati* is ready to be served.

13. Some people like to brush their *chappatis* with a little butter or *ghee* at this stage. Do not be disheartened if the *chappati* does not inflate as promised. Continue to follow the procedure, and it will cook properly. Taste the first *chappati* to see where you stand.

With a little experience, you will improve by leaps and bounds. Wipe the griddle between *chappatis* (to remove leftover dry flour) with a damp cloth. A delicious aroma will fill your kitchen as the aroma of freshly baked bread will do. The *chappati* is not a yeast bread, so this aroma is different, but just as appetizing.

14. Serve hot.

*Makes 10 **chappatis,** each about 4½ inches in diameter*

Paratha

*I*deal for improvisation! You can make it plain, or stuff it with vegetables. Even if you make it plain, you may add a pinch each of all, or any, of the following to the flour prior to making the dough: salt, anise seeds (whole or ground), whole fennel seeds.

Plain

1 cup whole wheat flour
About ½ cup water (as with *chappatis*; see page 42)
About 5 teaspoons *ghee*, melted
A small bowl of extra flour for rolling out *parathas*
About 3 teaspoons extra *ghee* for crispy style *parathas*

Note: A word about the *ghee*. There is no exact amount essential to the formation of a *paratha*. I have indicated approximate amounts. You may like more or less. Or you may not want *ghee* at all. In that case, butter-flavored vegetable shortening is a good substitute. Oil is not a good medium for *parathas*. Shortening, butter, or *ghee* are the best.

When preparing the dough, follow the same procedure as you would for *chappatis*, up to the point at which you cut the pieces for the balls. Since *parathas* are thicker than *chappatis*, you must cut 5 pieces instead of 10. When rolling out the *parathas* keep the same instructions in mind for the dough that you do when rolling out the *chappatis* . . . spread them out, cover them, etc.

Parathas can be made in the following shapes:

1. Triangular (Figure 3, page 47): Make a ball of the dough as you would for the *chappatis* and flatten it with three fingers. Pat both sides down in the extra flour. Then, on a flat surface, roll out the flattened dough ball into a round shape about 4 inches in diameter. Place ¼ teaspoon *ghee* in the center and spread it gently with your fingertips, well within the outer edges of the rolled dough. Pick up one edge of the round and bring it over the other side, so that you have folded it in half, with the *ghee* side inside. Now you have a half moon shape in front of you. Then fold the half moon in two, making it into a triangular shape. With the help of a little flour, roll out a triangular *paratha* with all sides the same length, about 5½ inches. Use the principle of rolling out a little at a time so that all sides are rolled out evenly, using a backward and forward movement.

2. Square (Figure 4, page 48): Follow the procedure for triangular *parathas* up to the stage at which you have spread the *ghee* in the center. Then, take one edge and bring it down over the *ghee*, a little inside the edge (as shown in the picture). Press down gently. Repeat with the opposite side and press down this edge over the previously folded edge. Repeat with the top and bottom, so that you have folded it like a square envelope, although the folds will overlap a great deal more than do the folds of an envelope. All these folds make the *paratha* layered, quite light and delicious. With the help of a little flour, roll out one side at a time, until each side is about 5½ inches and you have a square-shaped *paratha*.

3. Round (Figure 5, page 48. Instead of stuffing you will place *ghee* inside): Follow the same procedure as for triangular *parathas* up to the point at which you have spread the *ghee* in the center. Then, lift all the edges, and press together over the *ghee* portion, pressing hard with your fingers to make them stick together, forming a pouch with the *ghee* inside. Press the pouch down and with the help of a little flour roll out into a round *paratha* about 5½ inches in diameter.

4. So much for the shape. Now for the taste. Depending on your preference, you can make *parathas* soft or crisp.

SOFT STYLE: Heat a pancake griddle on medium heat for 10 minutes. Reduce heat to low. Place the *paratha* on the griddle. After a minute, flip it over. Take care to regulate

BELAN

Figure 1

"COOKIE" ROLL

Figure 2

TRIANGULAR *PARATHA*

Figure 3

SQUARE *PARATHA*

Figure 4

Rolled out dough   Side view   With stuffing   Gather edges above stuffing

Fold & press together   Press down

STUFFED *PARATHA*

Figure 5

the heat so that the *paratha* cooks well and does not burn outside or remain undercooked inside.

Cook for another minute and flip it over again.

Cover the *paratha* with a domed lid from a saucepan (Figure 6, this page). The dome need not be higher than an inch. This way you form a mini oven in which the *paratha* is well cooked inside and out. A friend of mine taught me how to make grilled cheese sandwiches like this. Cook this way for half a minute on either side.

You have first toasted the *paratha* and then baked it. Remove from griddle and set aside after brushing half a teaspoon *ghee* on top. When you make the next *paratha*, place it on top of the first *paratha*, on the side on which you had brushed the *ghee*. Then brush the *ghee* on top of the second *paratha*. Repeat this procedure till all the *parathas* are made. Indians do not mind having their *parathas* "buttered" on both sides!

CRISP STYLE: Follow the above procedure up to the point where you are to cover the *paratha* with a lid. Instead of covering the *paratha* with a lid, pour ½ teaspoon of *ghee* around the *paratha*, just as you would with pancakes. Lift the *paratha* for a second with a spatula, so that the *ghee* spreads evenly on the underside. After half a minute, flip the *paratha* over and repeat the procedure with the *ghee*.

PANCAKE GRIDDLE WITH DOMED SAUCEPAN LID

Figure 6

You have first toasted the *paratha* and then fried it on both sides.

It is a good idea to check the first *paratha* to be sure of the time required to cook it. If you feel the dough inside is undercooked, prolong the toasting stage by half a minute on both sides.

You must taste the first *paratha* to get a good idea of the heat and time required for cooking. All this sounds quite complicated. However, once you have done it, it is as simple as frying an egg. If you were to learn about frying eggs from a cookbook without ever having seen them being cooked, the instructions would be as detailed! When you fry *parathas*, there may be some spattering and smoking from the *ghee*. Remember always to wipe the griddle with a damp cloth after making each *paratha* to remove any flour that may remain on it.

Serve hot!

Makes 5 plain **parathas**

Stuffed *Paratha* à la New Delhi

These are parathas *stuffed with grated fresh cauliflower and spices. You may substitute finely minced onions or boiled, drained, coarsely mashed potatoes, and add the seasonings indicated for the cauliflower. The essential thing to remember is that the stuffing should be absolutely dry, without liquid or gravy, or else the* paratha *will not seal properly when you make a pouch of it. A stuffed* paratha *is usually crisp outside and soft inside. I know of few things that make a winter's day come alive so well as a well-made stuffed* paratha *and pickles.*

Stuffing

1 cup grated cauliflower
1 tablespoon grated fresh ginger
½ cup chopped fresh coriander
1 finely chopped medium onion
¼ teaspoon ground cumin seeds
¼ teaspoon ground coriander seeds
Salt to taste

To make dough

1 cup whole wheat flour
About ½ cup water (as with *chappatis*; see page 42)
⅛ teaspoon ground anise seeds
A small bowl of extra flour for rolling out breads
8 to 10 teaspoons *ghee* (page 24)

1. Mix well all the ingredients for the stuffing and set aside for an hour at room temperature. Make the dough for the *parathas* with the flour, water, and anise. The method is the same as that for *chappatis*. Set aside for an hour at room temperature before preparing the *parathas*.

2. When ready to make the *parathas*, squeeze the water from the stuffing and drain. The stuffing should be as dry as possible.

3. Next, follow the procedure for making *chappatis* up to the point at which you have to cut the dough roll. Since stuffed *parathas* are thicker than plain *parathas*, cut the roll into 4 pieces.

4. Then, make 4 balls of the pieces of dough, as you would for *chappatis*. Flatten each ball with three fingers, and pat down both sides on the extra flour. Then, on a flat surface, roll out the flattened dough ball into a round shape, about 4 inches in diameter. Place ¼ teaspoon *ghee* in the center and spread it gently with your fingertips, well within the outer edges of the rolled out dough.

5. Next, take ¼ cup (or enough to close the pouch comfortably) of the stuffing and place it in the center of the circle, taking care to see that the edges are free of *ghee* and stuffing. Fold by picking up all the edges of the circle and pressing them together above the vegetables, making a pouch as you would for the circular *paratha* (Figure 5, page 48). You may have to pull up the edges a bit. Press the edges together hard to make them inseparable. Gently flatten the pouch with the tips of your fingers, and sprinkle a little flour on top of it. Turn over and sprinkle some flour on the other side, too. Turn it over again so that the "pressed-together" side will be up. Gently applying the least possible pressure, roll out the *paratha* to about 5½ inches in diameter. Sprinkle a little more flour on the *paratha*, if necessary, to prevent tearing. The stuffed *paratha* is about twice as thick as the plain *paratha*, but it is the same diameter.

6. If you plan to make the *parathas* all at the same time, spread them out on a tray to prevent them from becoming one solid mass.

7. When ready to cook the *parathas*, heat a pancake griddle on medium heat for about 10 minutes. Reduce the heat to low and place the *paratha* on it.

8. After one minute, turn over and cook on the other side for one minute. Turn over and cover with a lid, and cook this way for a minute or so on both sides, till done.

9. For soft *parathas*, proceed as you would for soft plain *parathas*. For crisp *parathas*, fry as you would for crisp plain *parathas*.

10. Serve hot!

Makes 4 stuffed **parathas**

Saryu's Alltime *Puris*

*P*uffed, *deep fried breads*

1 cup whole wheat flour
About ½ cup water (as with *chappatis*; see page 42)
A pinch of salt
2 cups of oil for deep frying the *puris*
A few teaspoons of extra oil for rolling out the *puris*

1. Mix well all the ingredients, *except* the last two. Knead until the dough becomes stiff. This should take a few minutes, less in a food processor. The dough should not be elastic; rather, it should tear when you pull a piece off.

2. Set aside for a couple of hours at room temperature.

3. When ready to fry, make a roll and cut it into 12 pieces. (See *chappatis*, page 42.)

4. Make balls of the 12 pieces as you would for *chappatis*. Spread a few drops of oil on the counter and then roll out the *puris*. With the help of the oil, roll out the *puris* into flat round shapes about 3½ inches in diameter. Follow the same method for rolling out the *puris* as you would for *chappatis*, with the difference that you will use oil instead of flour.

5. Prepare all the *puris* beforehand, since it takes only a jiffy to fry them once the oil is ready. Remember to spread them out on a tray and cover them as you would the *chappatis*, as you will fry the *puris* one at a time.

6. Heat 2 cups oil in a wok on high heat.

7. It is crucial that the oil for deep frying the *puris* be at the right temperature, i.e., very hot, otherwise they will not inflate. A well-fried *puri* is almost round like a ball. A little experience in this, as in all else, is the best guide. Whatever you do, please use common sense in regulating the heat. The oil should be hot, but not dangerously so! One method of checking whether the oil is hot enough is to put a pinch of dough into the wok. If it rises to the top, sizzling, the oil is ready.

8. When you think the oil is ready, slide one *puri* into it, without splashing the oil!

9. Pour oil continuously onto the *puri* from the sides so that it is being fried from above and below. The *puri* should fry briskly. If the oil just simmers without any change in the appearance of the *puri*, the oil is not hot enough.

10. Fry the *puri* for about 15 seconds on one side. Turn over carefully with a round slotted frying spoon and fry for about 5 seconds. Lift with the spoon and hold it above the oil for a couple of seconds to drain off excess oil. Transfer to a large bowl or tray lined with paper towels. The towels will soak up the excess oil from the *puri*.

The first *puri* should give you a good idea of the time required to fry the *puris*. It should be a light, or golden, brown. Fry all the *puris* the same way, and transfer them to a paper-towel lined dish.

Puris can be eaten with vegetables and *dals* and go particularly well with potato curries.

Serve hot or cold.

Makes 12 **puris**

Non-Vegetarian

Chicken Curry à la Mussoorie

This creamy chicken should melt in the mouth.

2 medium onions, coarsely chopped
4 cloves garlic
1 tablespoon chopped fresh ginger
2 tablespoons water
¾ cup *ghee* (page 24)
1 teaspoon whole cumin seeds
2 small frying chickens, cut up
   (The elimination of pieces with bone reduces the flavor of a curry
   considerably. You could substitute thighs and drumsticks if you like,
   but avoid using boned breast of chicken. Remove skin, and clean chicken
   with dry paper towels before cooking.)
1 teaspoon ground turmeric
¼ teaspoon ground cayenne pepper
½ teaspoon ground cumin seeds
1 teaspoon ground coriander seeds
6 crushed cardamoms
1 medium cinnamon stick, crushed
2 bay leaves
Salt to taste
A pinch of nutmeg
1 pint sour cream
2 tablespoons blanched slivered almonds
1 cup chopped fresh coriander

1. Puree the onions, garlic, ginger, and 2 tablespoons of water in a blender.

2. In an 8-quart saucepan, heat the *ghee* on medium high heat. When the *ghee* is hot, add the whole cumin, stirring briskly until the seeds sizzle. Add the puree and continue to stir. Regulate the heat to prevent the puree from sticking to the bottom of the pan, which it has a tendency to do. Continue stirring till the puree is golden, has been fried well, and most of the moisture in the puree has evaporated. This will take about 10 minutes on medium high heat.

3. Add the chicken. Stir fry on high heat till the chicken starts turning golden brown. This should take about 5 minutes. Stir fry briskly to prevent burning the chicken. Add the turmeric, cayenne pepper, cumin, coriander, cardamom, cinnamon, bay leaves, salt, and nutmeg, stirring well until they give off a fragrance; i.e., for a minute or so. Add the sour cream, stirring constantly. Bring to a boil, reduce the heat to lowest point possible, cover tightly, and cook for 30 minutes or until the chicken is absolutely tender.

4. Just before serving, sprinkle almonds, and then fresh coriander, on the curry.

5. Serve hot.

Serves 6

Tandoori Chicken

This is a spectacular way to serve chicken. For those who like it spicy, it can be spiced up by doubling, or tripling, the amount of red cayenne pepper.

2 whole, small frying chickens
1 medium onion, coarsely chopped
1 tablespoon finely chopped fresh ginger
4 cloves garlic
½ cup plain, whole milk yoghurt
1 teaspoon ground cayenne pepper
Salt to taste
¼ cup lemon juice
3 tablespoons *garam masala* (page 23)
4 tablespoons *ghee* (page 24)

1. Remove the skin from the chickens. With a sharp knife, make 3 parallel slits on the fleshy parts. The slits should be bone deep and about 3 inches long. Do not worry if the chicken looks torn up. This way it absorbs the marinade better.

2. Puree the onion, ginger, garlic, yoghurt, cayenne pepper, salt, lemon juice, and 2 tablespoons of the *garam masala* together in a blender. This is the marinade.

3. Rub the marinade into the chickens, well into the slits and the rib cage from inside, so that the chickens are completely marinated. Keep in the refrigerator overnight for the best flavor. If you are in a hurry, marinate for at least 10 hours! In any case, you must turn the chickens a couple of times while marinating, so that they are well marinated inside and out, top and bottom.

4. Preheat the oven to 500°F. for 15 minutes.

5. Place the chickens in a roasting pan or dish. Sprinkle the remaining *garam masala* on the birds, and place in the oven. After 10 minutes, lower the heat to 400°F., put 2 tablespoons of *ghee* on each chicken, and cook for 50 minutes until done. Do not pour the leftover marinade on the chicken or even baste the chicken with the marinade, since that will make it soft. *Tandoori* chicken has to be crisp. That is why the oven has to be really hot to singe and seal the chicken and to prevent the juices from flowing out. Traditionally, *tandoori* chicken is made with a whole chicken, but if you prefer, you can use thighs and drumsticks. Naturally these take less time to cook than a whole chicken, but the temperatures required for cooking are the same.

6. Serve at once!

Serves 6

Sudha Koul

Piaz Chicken

Chicken in onion gravy

5 tablespoons oil
4 cups chopped onions
6 small chicken legs and thighs (12 pieces, if cut at the joint)
8 cardamoms, crushed well
2 medium cinnamon sticks
Salt to taste
⅓ cup water

1. Heat oil in a 4-quart saucepan on high heat. Add the onions, and fry until golden. Add the chicken. Fry until the chicken begins to brown a little. Add the cardamom and cinnamon, salt and water. Stir well, lower heat to medium, cover, and cook for about 20 minutes. Then remove the cover, turn up the heat to high, and stir and cook until the liquid is reduced to a thickish gravy. This should take a few minutes.

2. Serve hot.

Serves 6

Whispering Windows Butter Chicken

Chicken cooked with a buttery gravy . . . a very popular restaurant item

12 chicken thighs
1 cup plain, whole milk yoghurt
Salt to taste
¼ pound (1 stick) butter
1 big onion, finely minced
1½ teaspoons ground cumin seeds
1½ teaspoons ground coriander seeds
1½ teaspoons ground cayenne pepper
1 cup strained tomatoes
½ cup heavy cream
½ cup cashew nuts, ground
1 teaspoon cardamom seeds, crushed well

1. Remove skin from chicken. Make 2 parallel slits in each piece. Marinate overnight in yoghurt and salt.

2. When ready to cook, heat the butter in a 6-quart saucepan on medium high heat.

3. Add the onion and stir fry till golden, but not brown. Add the cumin, coriander, cayenne pepper, tomatoes; stir well. Add the marinated chicken, with the marinade. Reduce heat to medium. Stir. Cook covered for 15 minutes.

4. Add the cream, cashews, and cardamom; stir well. Cover and cook for 45 minutes, stirring occasionally.

5. Serve hot.

Serves 6

White Rondo à la Turk *Shami*

*R*ounds of ground turkey (or lamb), cooked in a delicately seasoned yoghurt gravy

2 pounds finely ground turkey or lamb
1 teaspoon cardamom seeds
Salt to taste
1 tablespoon ground fennel seeds
2 teaspoons ground cumin seeds
1½ teaspoons ground coriander seeds
2 tablespoons oil
2 teaspoons ginger powder
6 cloves
1¼ cups water
4 tablespoons oil
1 cup chopped onion
1 tablespoon finely chopped fresh ginger
1½ cups plain, whole milk yogurt
A pinch of saffron, soaked in a tablespoon of water
¼ teaspoon cardamom seeds, powdered

1. Mix well the following: Ground turkey or lamb, cardamom seeds, salt, fennel, cumin, coriander, 2 tablespoons oil, and ginger powder. Knead well for a minute or so. Divide into three equal portions. Make each portion into a roll about 6 inches long and about 2 inches in diameter, patting the rolls to help shape them. Place the meat "logs" or rolls in a heavy 6-quart saucepan. Add the cloves and water and bring to a boil over high heat. Cover, lower heat to medium, and continue to cook until the rolls are cooked and firm. This should take about half an hour. Remove from heat and allow to cool before placing in the refrigerator for a couple of hours.

2. When chilled, remove from the refrigerator. Remove the rolls from the saucepan. Reserve the liquid in the saucepan. Slice the rolls into half-inch-thick slices. Set liquid and rolls aside.

3. Heat the oil in a small frying pan, or saucepan, on high heat. Add the onion and fresh ginger, and fry until reddish. Add to the liquid in the saucepan.

4. Bring the contents of the saucepan to a boil.

5. Add the yoghurt; stir briskly. Add the slices of ground meat roll. Add the saffron.

6. Bring to a boil again. Add the powdered cardamom. Lower to medium, cover, and cook for 10 minutes.

7. Serve hot.

Serves 6

Kofte/Machh/Meatballs

Red hot meatball curry!

2 pounds lean ground meat
2 teaspoons ground cayenne pepper
5 tablespoons oil
1 teaspoon sugar
1 teaspoon ginger powder
2 teaspoons ground fennel seeds
1 tablespoon whole fennel seeds
1 teaspoon whole cumin seeds
1 tablespoon cardamom seeds
Salt to taste
1 medium onion, chopped
4 cloves
½ cup plain, whole milk yoghurt
1½ cups water
¼ teaspoon each: ground cardamom seeds, ground cumin seeds, ground
   cinnamon

1. Spread the ground meat on a large plate. Sprinkle 1 teaspoon of the cayenne pepper on the meat.

2. Heat 2 tablespoons of the oil in a small, heavy saucepan until it starts to smoke a little. Pour over the meat. Add the sugar, ½ teaspoon of the ginger powder, 1 teaspoon of the ground fennel, whole fennel, whole cumin seeds, cardamom seeds, and salt.

3. Knead together for a couple of minutes until all the ingredients are well mixed.

4. Now shape the meatballs. Traditionally, in Kashmir, these are made slightly elongated, like link sausages of a medium size. However, you could, if you prefer, make them round. Set meatballs aside.

5. Heat the remaining oil in a heavy 6-quart saucepan on medium high heat. Add the chopped onion and immediately thereafter the cloves, and fry till golden brown.

6. In the meanwhile, mix well the remaining cayenne pepper with the yoghurt. When the onions are a golden brown, add the cayenne pepper–yoghurt mixture. Stir fry briskly for a couple of seconds. Some rather pungent aromas emanate at this stage. People have been known to yearn for these aromas!

7. Add the water and remaining ground fennel and ginger; stir briskly until the mixture boils.

8. Add the meatballs, one at a time. Reduce heat to low, cover, and cook for about half an hour or until the meatballs become firm and are well cooked and the oil has risen to the top of the liquid in the saucepan.

9. Once you have placed the meatballs in the saucepan, do not stir until they have become firm. You could lift the saucepan and gently turn it about so that the gravy spreads well around the meatballs, but this need not be done more than once, if at all.

10. Once the meatballs are cooked and are firm, stir gently. Sprinkle the ground cardamom, cumin, and cinnamon on the meatballs, stir a little to mix well with the gravy, cover, and cook on low heat for another 5 minutes.

11. Serve hot.

Reheat on low heat till it starts simmering. It reheats deliciously.

Makes about 20 meatballs

Khulla Keema

Ground meat cooked with eggs, peas, and spices

1 medium onion, chopped coarsely
2 teaspoons chopped fresh ginger
4 cloves garlic
2 tablespoons water
¾ cup oil
½ teaspoon whole cumin seeds
2 pounds ground meat (lamb, beef, or turkey)
1 tablespoon ground cumin seeds
1 teaspoon ground cayenne pepper
2 tablespoons ground coriander seeds
½ tablespoon ground turmeric
20-ounce packet of frozen peas
Salt to taste
3 hard boiled eggs, halved
4 tablespoons heavy cream
1 teaspoon cardamom seeds, crushed
2 medium cinnamon sticks, crushed
½ cup water
½ cup chopped fresh coriander

1. Puree the onion, ginger, garlic, and 2 tablespoons of water in a blender.

2. Heat the oil on high heat in a 4-quart saucepan. Add the whole cumin seeds, and stir fry for a couple of seconds. Add the puree, and stir fry till the puree acquires a golden color. Stir to prevent burning.

3. Add the ground meat and stir fry well, breaking up lumps, for about 5 minutes. Reduce heat to medium. Add the ground cumin, cayenne pepper, ground coriander, ground turmeric, peas, and salt. Stir fry for 2 to 3 minutes. Add the eggs, cream, cardamom, cinnamon, and water. Stir well, cover, and cook on medium heat for about 20 minutes. Sprinkle fresh coriander on top and serve.

Serves 6

Tikka Kababs

These are similar to shish kababs, so popular in the United States, but the marinade is spicier.

2 tablespoons *garam masala* (page 23)
2 tablespoons lemon juice
1 small onion
1 tablespoon chopped fresh ginger
5 cloves garlic
1 teaspoon ground cayenne pepper, or more, to taste
Salt to taste
4 tablespoons sour cream
2 pounds boneless lamb (preferably from butterflied leg of lamb),
    cut in 2-inch cubes

1. Puree all the ingredients, *except* the lamb, together in a blender.

2. Pierce the cubes of lamb with a thick skewer or sharp knife, so that a visible hole is made in the meat. The idea is to allow the meat to marinate properly, which is the entire secret of this recipe. Marinate overnight in the refrigerator.

3. When you are ready to cook, place the kababs in a broiler pan to drain off excess juices.

4. Heat the oven to a full broil for 15 minutes.

5. Place the kababs in the oven. Broil for 15 minutes. Remove from the oven; turn pieces over. Broil for another 15 minutes.

6. Serve at once.

7. Sliced onions (marinated for a couple of hours in vinegar, a dash of cayenne pepper, and salt) are a good accompaniment. You may also serve a quartered lemon on the side of the kababs, if you wish.

Tandoori chicken and *Tikka* kababs can also be cooked on an outdoor grill. However, outdoor grills being different, you will have to use a little independent judgment about time and temperature. I find that *Tikka* kababs taste more authentic when cooked on the grill.

Serves 6

My Mother-in-Law's *Yakhni* for All Seasons

A mild, aromatic lamb curry

2 pounds fresh lean lamb shoulder, sliced
2 cups water
6 cloves
1 teaspoon ground cumin seeds
1 teaspoon ginger powder
2 teaspoons ground fennel seeds
3 bay leaves
1 cup plain, whole milk yoghurt
2 tablespoons sour cream
4 cardamom pods, coarsely crushed
Salt to taste
1 tablespoon *ghee* (page 24)
1 medium onion, minced
1 tablespoon finely chopped fresh ginger
A pinch of saffron

1. In a 4-quart saucepan, bring the lamb, water, cloves, cumin, ginger powder, fennel, and bay leaves to a boil on high heat. Reduce the heat to medium, cover, and cook the lamb until it is tender. This should take about 35 minutes.

2. There should be about half a cup of water left when the lamb is finished cooking. A little more won't hurt, but if the water dries up while the lamb is cooking, add half a cup of water to it. Stir once or twice to ensure that the lamb does not stick to the pan and burn. Mix the yoghurt and sour cream. Add to the lamb, stir well, and raise heat to medium high. Bring to a boil. Add cardamom and salt. Remove from heat and set aside.

3. In a separate pan, heat the *ghee* on high heat.

4. Add the onion and ginger, and stir fry until golden brown. Add to the lamb. Next, add saffron to the lamb, stir, cover, and cook lamb on low heat for about 10 minutes.

5. Remove the saucepan from the heat and let it rest for 5 minutes before serving.

Yakhni improves in flavor if kept overnight! Reheat on low heat till it starts simmering.

6. Serve hot.

Serves 4

Anu's Melt-in-the-Mouth *Bhuna* Lamb

Lamb cubes cooked in a rich, aromatic marinade

2 cups plain, whole milk yoghurt
8 cloves garlic
1 tablespoon chopped fresh ginger
1 teaspoon ground red pepper
1 teaspoon *garam masala* (page 23)
1 teaspoon ground coriander seeds
1 teaspoon ground cumin seeds
2 teaspoons lemon juice
Salt to taste
2½ pounds boneless lamb shoulder cut into 1½-inch cubes
1 tablespoon oil

1. Puree all the ingredients, *except* the lamb and oil.

2. Marinate the lamb in the puree for 4 to 5 hours in the refrigerator.

3. Place the meat, with the marinade, in a heavy 6-quart saucepan. Bring to a boil on medium high heat. Lower heat to medium, cover, and simmer for half an hour, until the lamb is tender.

4. Continue to cook uncovered until most of the moisture has evaporated and the lamb is thickly coated with the gravy. Add 1 tablespoon oil, and stir fry for 2 minutes.

5. Serve at once.

Serves 6

Sag Goshth

Meat curry in a rich, creamy spinach puree

One 10-ounce packet of fresh spinach
6 cups water
1 large onion, coarsely chopped
4 cloves garlic
1 tablespoon chopped fresh ginger
2 tablespoons water
½ cup oil
8 cloves
2 pounds lean lamb, such as lean sliced shoulder of lamb,
   cut into approximately 2″ × 3″ × 2″ pieces
2 medium tomatoes, coarsely chopped
1 teaspoon ground cayenne pepper
½ teaspoon ground turmeric
½ teaspoon ground cumin seeds
1 cinnamon stick, coarsely crushed
½ cup sour cream
½ teaspoon cardamom seeds, crushed
Salt to taste

1. Wash and drain spinach. Place spinach in a 6-quart saucepan. Add 6 cups of water. Boil for 3 minutes. Remove from heat. Cool.

2. Reserve the spinach and one cup of the liquid. Discard the rest of the liquid. Puree the spinach and the cup of liquid in a blender. Set aside.

3. Puree the onion, garlic, and ginger with 2 tablespoons of water.

4. In a 4-quart saucepan, heat the oil on high heat. Add the cloves and the onion puree. Stir fry briskly for 2 minutes, until the puree starts turning brown. Add the meat, and continue to fry briskly for 2 minutes. Lower heat to medium high, and continue frying until the meat starts browning. This should take a couple of minutes.

5. Add the tomatoes, cayenne pepper, turmeric, cumin, cinnamon, sour cream, cardamom, and salt. Stir fry well for a few seconds, and bring to a boil.

6. Add the spinach puree; stir. Reduce heat to the lowest point. Cover. Cook this way until the meat is tender. This should take about 45 minutes.

7. Serve hot.

Serves 6

Kaliya

Lamb pieces cooked with yoghurt and turmeric

2 pounds lamb shoulder, sliced 2 inches thick
2 cups water
6 cloves
2 teaspoons ground turmeric
1 tablespoon ground fennel seeds
½ teaspoon ginger powder
½ cup plain, whole milk yoghurt
Salt to taste
3 tablespoons butter
¼ teaspoon ground cinnamon
½ teaspoon ground cumin seeds
6 cardamoms, crushed thoroughly

1. Divide each lamb slice into 2 pieces.

2. Bring the lamb, water, cloves, and turmeric to a boil on high heat. Mix the fennel and ginger in the yoghurt. Add to the lamb. Bring to a boil again.

3. Add salt. Reduce heat to low; cover and cook for about 40 minutes. Set aside.

4. Heat the butter on high heat. Add the cinnamon, cumin, and cardamom. Stir. Add to the lamb mixture.

5. Cook lamb for another 10 minutes on low heat.

6. Serve hot.

Serves 4

Roghanjosh

The ultimate Kashmiri lamb dish, roghanjosh is cooked in an aromatic red gravy made with ground cayenne pepper and yoghurt.

½ cup oil
8 cloves
1 medium onion, chopped
3 pounds leg of lamb, or shoulder, cut into chop-size pieces
½ cup plain, whole milk yoghurt
1 teaspoon chopped fresh ginger
2 tablespoons ground cayenne pepper
3 cups water
1 tablespoon ground fennel seeds
1 teaspoon ginger powder
Salt to taste
¼ teaspoon ground cinnamon
½ teaspoon ground cumin seeds
8 cardamoms, crushed well

1. Heat the oil in a heavy 6-quart saucepan on high heat for 3 minutes. Add the cloves and onion. Fry until the onion turns reddish. Add the meat. Fry until it starts to brown a bit. Add the yoghurt and ginger. Stir and fry, until the liquid from the yoghurt evaporates.

2. Remove from heat and quickly add the cayenne pepper, stir until the meat acquires a red color, add the water, and return saucepan to heat. Add the ground fennel, ginger, and salt. Bring to a boil. Reduce the heat to low. Cover and cook until the lamb is tender. This should take about 45 minutes. If, after 45 minutes, the lamb is still not tender and the water has evaporated, add another cup of water and cook for another 15 minutes or until done.

3. When the lamb is tender, add the cinnamon, cumin, and cardamom. Stir, cover, and cook for one minute.

4. Serve.

Serves 4 to 6

Shahi Mia's recipe for *Shahi Korma*

Spiced lamb legacy from the Moghuls

½ cup oil
2 large onions, sliced
2 tablespoons grated fresh ginger
5 cloves garlic, minced
3 bay leaves
4 pounds lamb or beef cubes
2 teaspoons ground coriander seeds
1 teaspoon ground cayenne pepper
½ teaspoon cardamom seeds, powdered
1 teaspoon *garam masala* (page 23)
Salt to taste
1 cup plain, whole milk yoghurt, well stirred
½ cup blanched slivered almonds
¼ cup heavy cream
A pinch of saffron soaked in 2 teaspoons water

1. Heat the oil in a 6-quart saucepan on high heat for 2 minutes.

2. Add and fry the onions, ginger, garlic, and bay leaves until the onions are brownish.

3. Add the meat and fry till it starts to brown. Next, add the coriander, cayenne pepper, cardamom, *garam masala*, and salt.

4. Stir fry well for a couple of minutes.

5. Add the yoghurt, stir, reduce the heat to low, cover, and cook until the meat is tender. This should take about half an hour.

6. Add the almonds, cream, and saffron with the water; stir, cover, and cook for another 5 minutes.

7. Serve.

Serves 8

Awadhi Piaza

A courtly concoction of onions, meat, and spices

½ cup oil
2 pounds sliced, not chopped, onions
8 cloves garlic, minced
1½ ″ × 1″ slice fresh ginger, chopped
1 medium tomato, chopped
20 peppercorns
10 cardamoms, lightly crushed
2 large cinnamon sticks
10 whole dry red peppers
1 teaspoon whole cumin seeds, lightly crushed
10 cloves
Salt to taste
3 pounds lamb cubes, about 1½ ″ × 1″ × 1″ pieces
½ cup plain, whole milk yoghurt, beaten

1. Heat the oil in an 8-quart saucepan on high heat for a couple of minutes. Add the onions, garlic, and ginger; stir fry until nicely browned. Then add the tomato, and stirring all the time, cook for about 2 minutes.

2. Add all the other ingredients *except* the lamb and yoghurt, and stir fry for another minute or so.

3. Add the meat, and stir fry for 5 minutes.

4. Add the yoghurt, stir, cover, reduce heat to medium, and cook until the meat is tender. This should take half an hour.

5. Serve.

Serves 8

An Everyday *Vindaloo*

A rich, peppery curry based in vinegar and freshly blended spices. Vindaloo is addictive! It is traditionally made with pork, but lamb and beef work just as well.

2½ pounds boneless pork, beef, or lamb cut into 2″ × 2″ × 1″ pieces
6 tablespoons vinegar
2 large onions, sliced
2 tablespoons chopped fresh ginger
6 cloves garlic, chopped
1 cup chopped fresh coriander
4 dry hot peppers
1 tablespoon whole cumin seeds
2-inch cinnamon stick, coarsely crushed
6 tablespoons oil
1 tablespoon ground turmeric
1 teaspoon ground black pepper
3 hot green peppers
Salt to taste
1 teaspoon sugar
½ teaspoon ground cloves
2 cups water

1. Marinate the meat in 2 tablespoons of vinegar for 4 hours in the refrigerator.

2. Blend the onions, ginger, garlic, coriander, hot peppers, cumin, and cinnamon with the remaining vinegar to make a paste. You may have to add a tablespoon or two of water to facilitate blending.

3. When ready to cook, heat the oil in a 6-quart saucepan on high heat. Add the puree, and reduce heat to medium high. Fry briskly for a couple of minutes.

4. Add the turmeric, ground black pepper, meat, and the marinade. Fry well for 10 minutes, taking care not to burn the meat. Stir briskly, constantly.

5. Add the green peppers, salt, sugar, cloves, and 2 cups of water. Stir, cover, reduce heat to medium, and cook for about 45 minutes, until the gravy thickens and the meat is completely tender.

6. Serve hot.

Serves 4 to 6

Jigri and Buttons' Unforgettable *Tandoori* Fish

⅓ cup vinegar
1 tablespoon chopped fresh ginger
4 cloves garlic
Salt to taste
1 tablespoon ground coriander seeds
1 tablespoon ground cumin seeds
1 tablespoon ground cayenne pepper
½ cup oil
2 pounds of any mild white fish fillets, cut into 2″ × 3″ pieces

1. Make a paste of the vinegar, ginger, garlic, salt, coriander, cumin, cayenne pepper, and oil in the blender.

2. Marinate the fish pieces in the paste for 4 hours in the refrigerator.

3. Turn the oven on to broil at the highest point. Place the fish pieces on a baking tray. Broil for about 10 minutes. Turn over on the other side, and baste with the liquid in the baking tray. Broil for about 7 minutes again.

4. Broiling time may differ, depending on the thickness of the fillets. Thick fish fillets suit this recipe admirably.

5. Serve hot, straight from the oven, and enjoy!

Serves 6

Chutney Broiled Fish

*F*ish broiled in coriander chutney batter

2 pounds of any mild white fish fillets, cut into 3″ × 3″ pieces
2 cloves garlic
2 cups chopped coriander leaves
4 hot green peppers
1 teaspoon whole cumin seeds
1 tablespoon chopped coconut
¾ teaspoon ground turmeric
⅓ cup lemon juice
½ cup oil
Salt to taste

1. Pat fish dry and set aside. Make a paste of all the other ingredients. Apply thickly on the fish, on both sides. Broil for 10 minutes on either side.

2. Serve very hot, straight from the oven.

Serves 6

Fish Curry in a Trice

Fish cooked in tomato and coriander

4 tablespoons oil
2 medium onions, chopped fine
2 cloves garlic, chopped
1 tablespoon chopped fresh ginger
3 medium tomatoes, chopped
2 tablespoons ground coriander seeds
2 teaspoons ground turmeric
Salt to taste
1 tablespoon ground cumin seeds
2 cups water
2 pounds of any mild white fish fillets, cut into 2″ × 3″ pieces
1 cup chopped fresh coriander

1. Heat the oil in a 6-quart saucepan on high heat. Add the onions, garlic, and ginger. Fry for 2 to 3 minutes.

2. Add all the other ingredients *except* the water, fish, and fresh coriander. Fry well.

3. Add the water. Bring to a boil.

4. Add the fish and the coriander, bring to a good boil again, cover, and cook on medium heat for 15 minutes.

5. Serve hot.

Serves 6

Machhere Jhol

An appetizing and delicate fish curry from the land of fish lovers, Bengal

2 large tomatoes, coarsely chopped
1 tablespoon ground turmeric
2 teaspoons ground cumin seeds
Salt to taste
2 cups water
1 cup oil
2 pounds of any mild white fish, in thick fillets, cut into 2″ × 2″ pieces
½ teaspoon mustard seeds
½ teaspoon whole cumin seeds
¼ teaspoon whole fennel seeds, lightly crushed
½ teaspoon black cumin seeds
¼ teaspoon fenugreek seeds

1. Gravy: In a 4-quart saucepan, bring the tomatoes, turmeric, ground cumin seeds, salt, and water to a boil. Set aside.

2. In a non-stick frying pan, heat the oil on high heat.

3. Fry the fish, 4 to 5 pieces at a time, until golden.

4. Lift fish from the frying pan and place it in the gravy.

5. Add the mustard seeds, cumin seeds, fennel seeds, black cumin seeds, and fenugreek seeds to the oil in the frying pan. Stir fry on high heat for a few seconds. Add the entire contents of the frying pan to the fish. Cook the fish on medium high heat for 10 minutes.

6. Serve hot.

Serves 4

Vegetarian

Paneer Do Piaza

Homemade cottage cheese cubes, deep fried, and cooked in a tomato onion gravy

To make *paneer*, or cottage cheese:

½ gallon whole milk
2 pounds plain, whole milk yoghurt
1 cup lemon juice

1. Bring the milk to a good boil on high heat in a heavy 8-quart saucepan.

2. Mix the yoghurt and lemon juice well. Pour into the boiling milk.

3. Stir at once, only once, gently and slowly. Shut off heat after a minute. The milk should curdle. The water should separate from the milk solids and should be a light yellow color. Cover and leave for half an hour.

4. Then, place a thin muslin-type material, such as a fine quality men's large handkerchief, over a large colander. Place the colander in a sink or over another 8-quart saucepan (Figure 7, page 92). Pour the curdled mixture into the cloth so that all the liquid drains off through the colander, leaving the cheese in the cloth. This should take a couple of minutes.

5. Next, run cold water over the cheese for a minute. Allow all the liquid to drain off. Then tie up the cheese in the cloth, very tightly, so that some more liquid is drained off (Figure 8, page 92). Hang the cheese in the cloth for half an hour to drain off any remaining moisture (Figure 9, page 92).

6. Next, place the cheese on its side, on a board, so that the knot is on the side. Place another board on it, and then a heavy weight on the board, to press and squeeze out any moisture that might still be left in the cheese.

7. After 30 minutes, gently open up the cloth and place the cheese on a cutting board. If it is still warm, leave it until it cools completely. Then you can cut it into cubes about 2″ × 2″ × 1″.

8. To fry *paneer*:

1 cup oil

9. Heat the oil on high heat in a non-stick frying pan. Fry the cubes of cheese until they are a light reddish color. When done, lift with a slotted spoon and place in a bowl.

10. Do 4 or 5 pieces at a time. If you place too many pieces in the frying pan at the same time, they may stick together. Set aside.

HANDKERCHIEF
ON COLANDER
COLANDER ON
SAUCEPAN

Figure 7

CHEESE TIED
UP IN
HANDKERCHIEF

Figure 8

HANGING CHEESE

Figure 9

11. To cook *Do Piaza*, or twice-onioned (twice-onioned is twice blessed!), *paneer*:

½ cup oil from the frying oil
2 cups chopped onions
1 teaspoon finely chopped fresh ginger
2 cloves garlic, minced
2 medium tomatoes, chopped
1 tablespoon ground cumin seeds
1 tablespoon ground coriander seeds
1 cup sliced onions
¼ teaspoon ground cayenne pepper
¼ teaspoon cardamom seeds, crushed
1 tablespoon *garam masala* (page 23)
4 cloves
A pinch of ground nutmeg
2 cups water
Salt to taste
Fried cheese from the previous recipe

12. Heat the oil in a 4-quart saucepan on high heat for 2 minutes. Add the chopped onions, ginger, and garlic. Fry until golden brown for about 5 minutes. Add all the remaining ingredients, *except* the cheese. Stirring occasionally, cook for about 5 minutes, until a thick sauce is formed. Add the fried cheese; stir gently to avoid breaking the cheese cubes. Lower the heat to medium, cover, and cook for about 20 minutes.

13. Serve hot.

Serves 8 to 10

Rasam from Geetha

An appetizer made with lentils and tomatoes

½ cup lentils (*dal*)
5 cups water
2 teaspoons *rasam* powder (from an Indian store)
½ teaspoon ground turmeric
½ teaspoon garlic flakes
¼ teaspoon tamarind paste
Salt to taste
3 medium tomatoes, chopped
1½ cups water
1 tablespoon *ghee* (page 24)
1 teaspoon mustard seeds
1 teaspoon whole cumin seeds
½ cup chopped fresh coriander

1. Cook the lentils in 3 cups of water in a covered saucepan until soft.

2. In a 4-quart saucepan, bring 2 cups of water, *rasam* powder, turmeric, garlic flakes, tamarind, salt, and tomatoes to a boil. Cook on medium high heat for 20 minutes.

3. Add the *dal* (lentils); cook for 3 minutes. Add 1½ cups of water, and continue to cook on medium high heat.

4. Heat up the *ghee*. Add the mustard and cumin seeds, fry for a few seconds, and add to the *dal*. Add the coriander, boil once, and serve piping hot.

Serves 6

Delicious Everyday *Dal*

1 cup lentils
6 cups water
Salt to taste
3 ripe, medium tomatoes, chopped
1 large onion, finely chopped
2 garlic cloves, minced
2 tablespoons finely chopped fresh ginger
4 tablespoons *ghee* (page 24)
1 teaspoon ground turmeric
1 teaspoon whole cumin seeds
2 dry red hot peppers
½ cup chopped fresh coriander

1. Bring all ingredients, *except* fresh coriander, to a boil on high heat. Reduce heat to low, and cook until the *dal* is tender. This should take 20 to 30 minutes, depending on which *dal* you use.

2. When *dal* is done, sprinkle coriander on top, stir, and serve hot.

Serves 4 to 6

Moong *Dal*

1 cup yellow split moong *dal*
1 teaspoon ground turmeric
6 cups water
3 hot green peppers, halved
4 cloves
1 tablespoon curry leaves
Salt to taste
4 tablespoons butter
½ teaspoon whole cumin seeds
2 cloves garlic, minced
1 tablespoon chopped fresh ginger

1. Bring the *dal*, turmeric, water, peppers, cloves, curry leaves, and salt to a boil on high heat. Lower heat to medium and cook till the *dal* is tender. This should take 20 to 30 minutes.

2. Heat the butter in a small saucepan on high heat. Add the cumin, garlic, and ginger; stir fry for 2 minutes. Add to the *dal*; stir; and cook on medium high heat for 2 minutes more.

3. Serve hot.

Serves 4 to 6

Moti Mahal Dal

2 cups whole *urad dal*
One 15-ounce can red kidney beans, washed in water and drained
8 cups water
6 tablespoons *ghee* (page 24)
4 hot green peppers, sliced
6 tablespoons heavy cream
½ cup tomato puree
1 onion, finely chopped
4 cloves garlic, finely chopped
1 tablespoon chopped fresh ginger
1 teaspoon whole cumin seeds

1. Bring the *dal*, beans, and water to a boil with 2 tablespoons *ghee* and half the sliced peppers. Reduce heat to medium and cook for about 45 minutes or until *dal* is tender.

2. Add the heavy cream. Let the mixture boil for a minute or so. Add the tomato puree and remove from heat.

3. In a frying pan, heat the remaining *ghee* on high heat.

4. Add the onion, garlic, ginger, remaining sliced peppers, and cumin and fry for a couple of minutes. Add to the *dal* and bring to a boil. Reduce heat to low and cook for 3 minutes.

5. Serve.

Serves 6

Razmah

Kidney beans for kings, made from the king of beans!

2 cups dry red kidney beans and
8 cups boiling water *or*
Three 15-ounce cans kidney beans, washed and drained, plus 1 cup water
2 tablespoons *ghee* (page 24)
1 teaspoon whole cumin seeds
1 cup sliced onions
2 cloves garlic, minced
1 tablespoon chopped fresh ginger
3 medium tomatoes, chopped
1 tablespoon ground cumin seeds
1 tablespoon ground coriander seeds
1 teaspoon ground turmeric
¼ teaspoon ground cayenne pepper
Salt to taste
3 hot green peppers
½ cup chopped fresh coriander

1. If you are cooking beans from scratch, clean and wash the beans. Place in a 4-quart saucepan. Pour the boiling water over the beans, and soak them in that water overnight.

2. The next day, bring the beans to a boil in the same water. Reduce heat to low, and cook to desired tenderness. This may take an hour or more. If the water dries up as you cook, you can add more water and cook until the beans are done. (This method is not required for canned beans.)

3. *Or* you can use the canned beans and the cup of water. From now on the procedure is the same for both types of beans. Set aside the beans.

4. In a 4-quart saucepan, heat the *ghee* on medium high heat.

5. Add the whole cumin seeds, and stir fry for a few seconds.

6. Add the onions, garlic, and ginger; fry until reddish. Add the tomatoes, ground cumin, ground coriander, turmeric, cayenne pepper, and salt; fry for a couple of minutes until a thick sauce is formed. Add the kidney beans and green peppers. Stir, bring to a boil, add the fresh coriander, and cook for 5 minutes.

7. Serve.

Serves 6 to 8

Curried Chick Peas from Ushaji

2 cups dry chick peas, soaked overnight in 4 cups water
4 more cups water *or*
Three 16-ounce cans chick peas (washed with cold water and drained), plus
   1 cup water
3 tablespoons oil
2 teaspoons whole cumin seeds
2 teaspoons crushed anise seeds
1 tablespoon ground coriander seeds
½ teaspoon ginger powder
4 black cardamom pods, crushed well
1 cup tomato puree
1 teaspoon tamarind paste
1 tablespoon dry mint powder
Salt to taste

1. For chick peas soaked in water: Bring the soaked peas with the water, plus the additional 4 cups of water to a boil in a 4-quart saucepan. Lower heat to medium, cover, and cook for an hour until tender.

2. *Or* use the canned chick peas plus the cup of water. From now on the procedure is the same for both types of chick peas.

3. Set aside the chick peas.

4. Heat the oil in a 4-quart saucepan, on high heat. Add all the other ingredients, *except* the chick peas.

5. Stir fry for a few seconds. Add the chick peas, bring to a boil, reduce heat to low, cover, and cook for 20 minutes.

6. Serve.

Serves 8

Garlic Cabbage from Calcutta

Lovely with hot chappatis *or rice!*

6 tablespoons oil
6 hot green peppers, finely chopped*
5 cloves garlic, minced
1 medium cabbage, washed and drained thoroughly, cut into thin strips as for cole slaw; the strips should be as long as possible
Salt to taste

1. In a 6-quart saucepan, heat the oil on high heat. Add the peppers and garlic, and stir fry briskly for a few seconds until golden. Add the cabbage and salt, and stir well until all ingredients are mixed thoroughly. This should take a couple of minutes.

2. Cook for 2 minutes. Turn off heat, and cover for 5 minutes before you serve. The cabbage should be a little crunchy when done, not raw and not too soft.

3. Serve at once.

Serves 6

*You may reduce the number of peppers for mildness, but at least 4 peppers, seeds and all, are required for this recipe.

Bhindi Aloo

Crisp, curried okra and potatoes

1 pound fresh okra
1 pound medium potatoes, cut like home fries, preferably red potatoes with skin left on
¾ cup oil
1 tablespoon ground coriander seeds
1 tablespoon ground cumin seeds
½ tablespoon ground turmeric
1 tablespoon *garam masala* (page 23)
Salt to taste
Optional: ½ cup chopped fresh coriander for seasoning

1. Wash and drain vegetables thoroughly. The okra, particularly, should be washed and drained well in advance so that it is completely dry when ready to be cooked. When the okra is completely dry, cut off and discard the stem ends.

2. Heat the oil in a heavy wok on high heat for a couple of minutes. Add the vegetables. Stir fry for about 5 minutes.

3. Add all the other ingredients, *except* the coriander, and stir well. Lower heat to medium, cover, and cook until potatoes and okra are done; i.e., tender.

4. Sprinkle with chopped coriander, if you like coriander as much as I do!

5. Serve.

Serves 6

Broccoli Rabe *Haak*

A quick, delicious, and nutritious recipe

1 pound broccoli rabe or rabi
6 tablespoons oil
½ teaspoon dry *hing* powder
Salt to taste
10 small dry hot red peppers
1½ cups water

1. Wash and cut rabe stalks in half. Remove any seeds or flowers.

2. Heat the oil in a 4-quart saucepan on high heat for a couple of minutes. Remove from heat.

3. Add the *hing*, salt, peppers, and water.

4. Return saucepan to heat.

5. Add rabe, stir, bring to a boil, lower heat to medium high, cover, and cook for 10 minutes.

6. Remove cover immediately after the 10 minutes are over to retain the appetizing green color of the leaves.

Serving suggestion for a different and refreshing taste: serve with hot boiled rice and plain yoghurt!

Serves 4

Hot Broccoli

5 tablespoons oil
1 tablespoon crushed peppers
Salt to taste
1 head of broccoli, washed, drained, cut into pieces, stalks and all

1. Heat the oil on high heat in a 4-quart saucepan for 2 minutes.

2. Add the peppers, salt, and broccoli. Stir fry for 2 minutes.

3. Reduce heat to medium high; cook, covered, for 5 minutes.

4. Serve.

Note: Turnips and kohlrabi can also be cooked this way. However, you may need to add a cup or two of water to the vegetables after stir frying, since they take longer to cook than broccoli.

Serves 4 to 6

Kalpana's *Dosa Bhaji*

Served as a potato filling for South Indian crepes called dosas, bhaji *is delightful even with rice or bread.*

4 tablespoons oil
1 teaspoon mustard seeds
1 teaspoon *channa dal*
1 teaspoon *urad dal*
3 cloves
10 curry leaves
2 tablespoons chopped fresh ginger
3 hot green peppers, coarsely chopped
2 small sliced onions
4 boiled, large potatoes, broken into chunks
Salt to taste
½ teaspoon ground turmeric
3 medium tomatoes, chopped
½ teaspoon ground cayenne pepper
1 cup water
¼ cup chopped fresh coriander

1. In a 4-quart saucepan, heat the oil on high heat for 2 minutes. Reduce heat to medium high.

2. Add the mustard seeds, and stir fry for a couple of seconds.

3. Add the *channa* and *urad dal,* and stir fry for a few seconds.

4. Add the cloves, curry leaves, ginger, green peppers, and the onions. Fry until the onions are soft. Add the potatoes; fry for a few more minutes.

5. Add the salt, turmeric, tomatoes, and cayenne pepper. Pour in the water; stir well. Reduce heat to medium, cover, and cook for about 10 minutes. Sprinkle the coriander on top.

6. Serve.

Serves 6

Eggplant and Tomato Curry

Try to use garden fresh baby eggplants for this preparation, which is very similar to a ratatouille.

3 medium tomatoes, very preferably those ripened on the vine
3 hot green peppers
1 teaspoon ground turmeric
½ teaspoon ginger powder
½ teaspoon ground fennel seeds
½ teaspoon ground cumin seeds
3 cloves
1 cup water
½ teaspoon ground cayenne pepper
Salt to taste
1 pound small or baby eggplants
1 cup oil

1. Gravy: Cut each tomato into 6 pieces. Place the tomatoes and all the other ingredients, *except* the eggplants and the oil, in a 4-quart saucepan. Cook on medium high heat for 5 to 7 minutes or until the tomatoes have cooked down a bit. Set aside.

2. Wash and wipe the eggplants dry so that when you fry them, there is very little splattering. Cut into quarters lengthwise. If the eggplants are long, cut into quarters lengthwise and then once across so that you have 8 pieces.

3. Heat the oil on high heat in a wok for a couple of minutes. Add the eggplants, and stir fry for about 5 minutes until the eggplants start turning a little reddish in places. Pour eggplants and oil into the tomato mixture. Stir a bit to cover eggplants with the gravy.

4. Return saucepan to heat, and cook uncovered on medium high heat for another 5 minutes.

5. Serve.

Serves 4 to 6

✽ ✽ ✽

Cauliflower and Peas Curry

¾ cup oil, or *ghee* (page 24)
½ teaspoon whole cumin seeds
2 medium onions, sliced
3 cloves garlic, minced
2 tablespoons finely chopped fresh ginger
3 medium tomatoes, chopped
2 teaspoons ground coriander seeds
1 teaspoon ground turmeric
2 teaspoons ground cumin seeds
1 teaspoon ground cayenne pepper
2 black cardamoms, crushed well
Salt to taste
1 medium cauliflower, cut into 3-inch-long florets, washed and drained
    thoroughly, so that it is dry
2½ cups frozen peas
1 cup chopped fresh coriander

1. Heat the oil or *ghee* on high heat in a wok. Add the whole cumin, and stir until it sizzles briskly for a few seconds. Add the onions, garlic, and ginger; stir fry till a golden brown. Add the tomatoes and continue frying for about 5 minutes until you have a reddish paste. Add the ground coriander, turmeric, cumin, cayenne pepper, cardamom, and salt; continue stir frying until all the spices are well blended in the paste. Add the cauliflower and fry well. This should take about 8 minutes on high heat. Stir off and on to prevent the mixture from sticking to the bottom of the wok.

2. Add the peas, stir, lower heat to medium high, cover, and cook till the cauliflower is done to desired tenderness. This should take about 5 minutes. Just before serving, sprinkle the fresh coriander on top.

3. Avoid using any water to cook cauliflower if you want it to be crunchy and not too soft. However, if you feel the gravy is drying up too fast and the cauliflower is likely to burn, add ¼ cup of water.

Serves 6

Green Beans Curry from Aruna, a Southern Belle

1 pound green beans, cut into 1-inch pieces
Salt to taste
½ cup water
2 tablespoons oil
½ tablespoon mustard seeds
A few curry leaves
½ tablespoon grated fresh ginger
1 small onion, finely chopped
½ cup grated fresh coconut

1. Bring the beans, salt, and water to a boil in a medium saucepan on high heat. Cover, lower heat to medium, and cook for 10 minutes. Drain off water and set the beans aside.

2. In a 4-quart saucepan, heat the oil on high. Add the mustard seeds, curry leaves, ginger, and onion. Fry for a couple of minutes. Add beans, and stir fry for a minute. Add the grated coconut, stir, and remove from heat.

3. Serve hot.

Serves 6

Tulli's *Dam Aloo*

Smothered whole potatoes in a yoghurt gravy

1 pound medium potatoes
Water to cover and boil potatoes
2 cups oil
1 medium onion, chopped
½ cup plain, whole milk yoghurt
1 teaspoon ground cayenne pepper
1 teaspoon ground fennel seeds
½ teaspoon ginger powder
¼ teaspoon ground cumin seeds
6 cloves
Salt to taste
1 cup water

1. Boil the potatoes in a saucepan until done. Drain off water. Allow potatoes to cool. Pare off skin and perforate potatoes all over, deeply, with a toothpick. Set potatoes aside. Heat the oil in a wok on high heat until very hot. Deep fry the potatoes until they become reddish brown all over. This may take a while. The potatoes are not done until they turn reddish all over. Remove with a slotted spoon and set aside. Remove wok from heat.

2. In a 4-quart saucepan, heat 3 tablespoons of the oil from the wok on medium high heat. Add the onion, and fry until light brown. Mix the yoghurt with the cayenne pepper and stir in with the onion. Add the fennel, ginger, cumin, cloves, and salt in quick succession; stir. Add the water, then the potatoes. Stir gently, but well. Bring to a boil. Cover. Reduce heat to low, and cook for 10 minutes.

3. Serve hot.

About 6 medium **dam aloo**

Raita

My Mother-in-Law's Fresh
Chugandhar Raita

*B*eetroot and yoghurt delight

4 medium beets, boiled, peeled, and diced
1 onion, finely chopped
1 hot green pepper, very finely chopped
1 tablespoon grated fresh ginger
Salt to taste
¼ teaspoon whole cumin seeds
¼ teaspoon ground black pepper
½ cup chopped fresh coriander; save a pinch for garnish
2 cups plain, whole milk yoghurt
1 pint sour cream

1. Wash beets thoroughly under running water to remove some of the color. Drain well.

2. Mix all the ingredients; garnish with a pinch of the fresh coriander.

3. Chill and serve.

Note: The yoghurt and sour cream acquire a glamorous pink color that really brightens up a dinner table.

Serves 6

Orange Cucumber *Raita*

1 cucumber
Salt to taste
2 cups plain, whole milk yoghurt
1 cup sour cream
One 15-ounce can mandarin oranges, drained
½ cup chopped fresh coriander

1. Wash and peel the cucumber; cut in half, lengthwise. Spoon out the seeds and discard them. Grate cucumber and sprinkle with salt. Set aside for an hour.

2. Mix the yoghurt and the sour cream well.

3. Add oranges. Squeeze out the water from the cucumber by hand.

4. Add the cucumber to the yoghurt mixture. Mix well.

5. Garnish with coriander.

6. Serve chilled.

Serves 6

Mint *Raita*

2 cups plain, whole milk yoghurt
½ cup sour cream
Mint chutney
A few fresh mint leaves

1. Mix well all the ingredients, *except* the mint leaves.

2. Garnish with the mint leaves, chill, and serve.

Serves 4 to 6

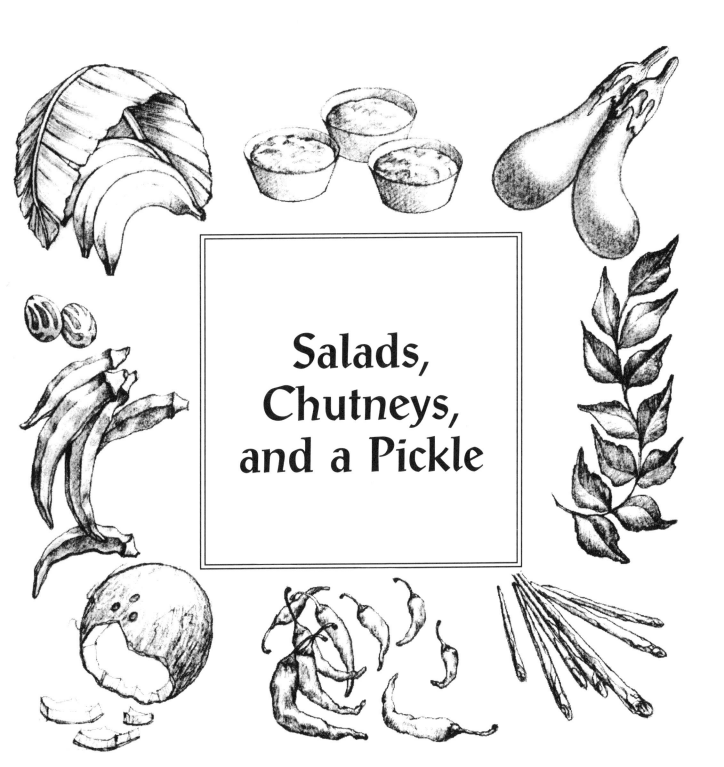

Salads, Chutneys, and a Pickle

Traditional Everyday Salad

This salad goes well with tandoori *meats.*

2 large onions, sliced
2 beets boiled until tender, cooled, peeled, and sliced
1 cucumber, peeled and sliced
1 large tomato, sliced
1 fresh lime, sliced
2 hot green peppers, sliced
6 scallions, cleaned, cut to 5" length, then halved lengthwise
2 tablespoons vinegar
Salt and pepper to taste

1. Place the onions in a layer on a large plate. Next, place the beets on top in a layer, then the cucumber, then the tomato slices, and last of all the sliced lime. Scatter the green peppers on top. Arrange the scallions in a pattern on the vegetables. Sprinkle with vinegar, salt, and pepper.

2. Chill and serve.

Serves 6 to 8

Mahavir *Ka Cachumber Ka Salaad*

A finely minced salad, cachumber *is a perfect accompaniment to a rich* pullao *or* biryani. *In fact, it can be the only other accompaniment, along with yoghurt, if you are in the mood for a light meal. The name* cachumber salaad *originates from the Indian chef's inability, presumably, to pronounce the Britisher's favorite salad vegetable, cucumber. Now* cachumber *means a finely chopped salad, and the word has found a place in verbal arguments in which the parties are threatening each other with dire consequences!*

1 large cucumber
1 large onion
1 large tomato
Salt to taste
1 tablespoon lemon juice
1 cup chopped fresh coriander

1. Dice the cucumber, onion, and tomato very fine by halving, then cutting into strips and then cutting across. Add the salt, lemon juice, and coriander. Mix well.

2. Chill and serve.

Serves 4 to 6

Mint Chutney

Refreshing!

Fresh mint, about 3 cups of leaves, washed
½ onion
1 tablespoon chopped fresh ginger
4 green hot peppers
Salt to taste
¼ cup lemon juice
A little water to blend, about 3 tablespoons

1. Grind all ingredients together in a blender.

2. Serve with kababs and *samosas.*

Serves 4 to 6

Saryu's Date Chutney

12 ounces pitted dates
2 tablespoons brown sugar
2 tablespoons tamarind paste
Pinch of salt
1½ cups water

1. Puree all the ingredients together in a blender.

2. Serve chilled or at room temperature.

Serves 4 to 6

Fresh Chutney

1 large ripe tomato
6 hot green peppers
2 cups chopped fresh coriander
1 small onion, coarsely chopped
2 cloves garlic
2 tablespoons lime juice
Salt to taste

SUDHA KOUL

1. Puree all the ingredients together in a blender.

2. Chill and serve.

Serves 4 to 6

Walnut Mint Chutney

1 dozen walnuts, shelled and soaked in water for 24 hours
2 hot green peppers
1 cup fresh mint leaves, washed and drained
⅓ cup water
Salt to taste
3 tablespoons sour cream (optional)

1. Grind all the ingredients together in a blender.

2. Chill and serve.

Note: For a variation, add 3 tablespoons of sour cream and mix well.

Serves 4 to 6

My Favorite Cooked Pickle

Sweet and sour, this pickle is almost like a curry!

1½ pounds raw mangoes or hot green peppers; very, very fresh, without any bruises
½ cup whole cumin seeds
¼ cup whole fenugreek seeds
1 cup wine vinegar
½ cup chopped fresh ginger
12 large cloves garlic
1 medium onion, coarsely chopped
1½ teaspoons salt
1 cup sugar
1 tablespoon ground cayenne pepper
1 cup oil

1. Wash the mangoes (or peppers), and dry them completely. Chop into small pieces and set aside.

2. Grind the cumin and fenugreek seeds well in the vinegar. Add all the other ingredients, *except* the oil and the mangoes (or peppers), and grind until a fine puree is made.

3. Heat the oil in a wok on high heat until it almost starts to smoke. Add the puree very carefully, and stir fry briskly for 3 to 4 minutes.

4. Add the mangoes (or peppers), and stir fry briskly for another 3 to 4 minutes. Remove from heat. Allow to cool completely.

5. Store in an airtight bottle in the refrigerator.

Note: Always use a clean, dry spoon when serving the pickle, as this keeps the pickle from spoiling.

Desserts

East Meets West in Mango Soufflé

An "exceptional" recipe from Lily

2 small envelopes unflavored gelatin
2 cups mango puree
A small pinch of saffron
4 egg whites
¼ cup sugar
½ pint heavy whipping cream
8 green pistachios, ground
Seeds of 2 cardamom pods, crushed to a powder

1. Stir the gelatin into 1 cup mango puree. Stirring all the time, cook over medium heat till the gelatin dissolves. Remove from heat. Add the saffron and the other cup of mango puree; stir well. Chill in the refrigerator, until mounds form in the puree when you lift it with a spoon. This should take about 15 minutes. Remove from refrigerator.

2. Whip up the egg whites with ¼ cup of sugar until stiff, and fold them into the puree.

3. Whip up the cream. Reserve a dollop for decoration. Fold the rest of the whipped cream into the mango puree. Pour into a glass dish.

4. Sprinkle with pistachios and cardamom. Top with the dollop of whipped cream.

5. Chill for at least 3 hours, or until it sets.

6. Serve.

Serves 8

Rasmalai à la Vini

Rasmalai, *translated literally, means cream sauce. This is a dessert made of cottage cheese, cream, sugar, and nuts. In India, the cheese is shaped into balls and soaked in cream after being cooked. Then it is chilled, garnished, and served. This delicious version is a shortcut.*

2 pounds ricotta cheese
½ cup sugar
1 pint half and half
A pinch of saffron
¼ teaspoon cardamom seeds, finely crushed
½ cup blanched almonds, finely slivered
2 tablespoons crushed green pistachios

1. Mix the cheese and sugar very well. Spread out on a deep 9″ × 12″ baking tray. Bake at 350°F. for 35 minutes or until it sets. It should not brown. Remove from oven. Cool at room temperature and cut into 2-inch squares. Place in a dessert bowl.

2. Mix the other ingredients, *except* the pistachios, well in a separate dish. Pour over the squares. Decorate with pistachios.

3. Chill for 2 to 3 hours before serving.

Serves 8

Kulfi Gali Wali

A centuries-old ice cream, courtesy of Ushi

One 12-ounce can evaporated milk
1 pint heavy whipping cream
One 14-ounce can condensed sweetened milk
2 slices white bread, edges trimmed
20 almonds, blanched and peeled
½ cup green pistachios
A pinch of saffron, soaked for 10 minutes in 1 teaspoon water
½ teaspoon cardamom seeds, crushed well

Put everything in the blender. Run the blender for about a minute until everything is well pureed. After turning off the blender, mix the ingredients with a spatula to make sure the nuts are not at the bottom. Run the blender once again for a minute. Make sure the nuts are well pureed with the other ingredients. Pour into popsicle molds. Freeze overnight or for at least 12 hours. Makes approximately 12 molds.

Serves 12

Ghulab (Rose) *Jamuns* from Geetha

"Rose Berries" in a fragrant syrup

4 cups water
1 tablespoon rose water
3 cups sugar
A pinch of saffron
2½ cups dry milk powder
½ cup all purpose flour
⅛ teaspoon baking soda
About 1½ cups heavy whipping cream, enough to make dough
About 50 cardamom seeds
2 cups oil

1. Bring the water, rose water, and sugar to a boil. Add the saffron. Remove from heat and set aside near the wok in which you plan to fry the *ghulab jamuns.*

2. Mix well the milk powder, flour, soda, and heavy cream. Knead until a soft dough is made. Take a teaspoon of the dough; place one cardamom seed in it and make a small ball.

3. Make balls with the rest of the dough similarly. Set aside. It is a good idea to make all the balls and then fry them in batches of 8. It takes a minute or two to fry the *jamuns* when the oil is ready.

4. In a wok, heat the oil on medium high heat for 10 minutes. When ready, fry the *ghulab jamuns*, until they turn brownish.

5. Remove with a slotted spoon and transfer to the syrup, which should still be quite warm. If, for some reason, the syrup has become entirely cold, heat it up a little before you place the *jamuns* in it.

6. This is a good recipe for the winter *and* summer. In the winter *ghulab jamuns* are usually served heated. In the summer they can be served chilled or at room temperature.

Makes about 50 **ghulab jamuns,** *about 3 to a serving*

Bhappa Doi, the Way Ammi Makes It

A steamed yoghurt dessert favorite from Bengal

One 14-ounce can condensed sweetened milk
1¼ cups plain, whole milk yoghurt
2 tablespoons blanched, slivered almonds
¼ teaspoon crushed cardamom
⅛ teaspoon ground nutmeg

1. Mix all the ingredients well and steam in a covered pan, about the size of a 9-inch pie dish, for about half an hour until the *doi* solidifies. Remove from heat, and set aside to cool. Next, chill in the refrigerator for at least 4 hours. When chilled, cut into 2-inch pieces.

2. Serve chilled. Two pieces or more to a serving.

Serves 6

Agha Shahid Ali's Easy-as-Pie *Khir*, or, a Shortcut to a Heavenly Rice Pudding

This amazingly simple and delectable version of khir *is a concoction of a friend of mine. His guests always rave over his* khir. *You have to try this recipe to find out why!*

½ cup good quality rice
5 cups water
One 12-ounce can evaporated milk
One 14-ounce can condensed sweetened milk
A pinch of saffron
6 crushed cardamom pods
1½ cups in all of almonds, Brazil nuts, cashew nuts, and dates, all finely slivered
½ cup raisins

1. Bring the rice and water to a boil. Reduce heat to the lowest point, cover, and cook until the rice is very soft and sticky. This should take about 30 minutes or so. Remove from heat. Set aside to cool.

2. When cool, mash with a potato masher.

3. Add all the other ingredients, mix well, and bring to a boil in a very heavy saucepan. Stir, lower heat to the lowest point, and simmer for 10 minutes.

4. Serve hot or chilled.

Serves 6

SUDHA KOUL

Nankatai or Indian Biscuits

8 ounces (2 sticks) butter
1½ cups sugar
2 teaspoons water
½ teaspoon baking soda
½ teaspoon cardamom seeds, powdered
2 cups all purpose flour
A few green pistachios, slivered

1. Soften butter at room temperature. Add the sugar, water, and soda. Blend this in a food processor until creamy.

2. Mix the cardamom with the flour well.

3. Blend the flour mixture, one tablespoon at a time, into the butter mixture, in a food processor till you achieve a soft, smooth dough.

4. Form into small balls by the spoonful, with the palms of your hands (see *chappatis*, page 42). Decorate each ball with a sliver of pistachio.

5. Preheat the oven to 300°F. When ready, place the *nankatai* on cookie sheets and bake like cookies for about 15 minutes. The *nankatai* are done when they start to turn a little brown at the bottom.

6. Remove from oven and allow to cool at room temperature. Enjoy!

Makes about 4 dozen nankatai

Snacks

Samosa

A standard snack at tea time. Samosa is a deep fried, spring roll type of savory, usually stuffed with potatoes and peas. Cooked, spiced ground meat can be used instead of potatoes.

For the dough:

2 cups all purpose flour
1½ teaspoons whole cumin seeds
¼ teaspoon ground anise
A pinch of salt
½ cup vegetable shortening
About ⅓ cup chilled water to make dough
½ cup extra flour to roll out the wrappers
2 cups vegetable shortening to deep fry the *samosas*

  1. Mix the flour, cumin, anise, and salt. Add the shortening, and rub into the flour mixture, until little granules are formed. Add the water, a little at a time, until a stiff dough is made. Knead well for a few minutes, cover, and keep in the refrigerator for a couple of hours before rolling out the wrappers.

  2. When ready to roll, make a "log" out of the dough, as described for *chappatis* (page 42). Cut into 10 pieces.

  3. Make a ball out of one piece with your palms, as you would for *chappatis*. Flatten the ball on the counter.

  4. With the help of a little dry flour, roll out a flat, round shape, about 7" in diameter. Follow the basic rules for rolling out the *chappatis*.

  5. With a knife or pizza cutter, cut the rolled out circle in half.

6. Take one half with the curved side toward you as indicated in Figure 10, page 141.

7. Place a tablespoon of the filling in the center (Figure 11, page 141).

8. Moisten the curved edges, by dipping your finger in water, and running over the edge.

9. Next, fold the right half over the filling (Figure 12, page 141). Moisten top edge.

10. Bring the left fold over the folded right half and press down gently (Figure 13, page 141).

11. Moisten the base of the triangle, fold up at the edge and top, and press down well with a fork or fingertips, as you do with pastry, to seal it (Figure 14, page 141). This ensures that the filling does not stand a chance of spilling out.

12. Make all the *samosas* and set them out on a tray.

13. To fry: Heat the 2 cups of vegetable shortening in a wok on high heat. Reduce heat to medium high.

14. When the shortening has been on medium high heat for 5 minutes, drop a pinch of dough into it. If the dough rises to the top at once, the oil is ready.

15. Deep fry the *samosas*, 4 at a time. Fry on one side until they turn a golden brown. Then turn them over, and fry on the other side.

16. When done, lift the *samosas* with a slotted spoon and place them on 3 to 4 layers of paper towels. The towels soak up excess oil.

Samosas can be eaten hot or cold. To reheat, warm *samosas* in the oven.

17. Serve with ketchup or chutney.

Figure 10

Figure 11

Figure 12

Figure 13

Figure 14

Filling for samosas:

6 medium potatoes, boiled until done, peeled, broken into coarse chunks
1 large onion, very finely chopped
2 tablespoons finely chopped fresh ginger
2 cloves garlic, minced
1 cup peas, frozen (or precooked by boiling and draining off the water)
1 teaspoon crushed red pepper, less to taste
2 tablespoons ground coriander seeds
1 teaspoon ground cumin seeds
2 cups chopped fresh coriander
Salt to taste

Note: Instead of the potato filling, you can use the cooked meat from the *Khulla Keema* recipe (page 69). All you need to add to the ground meat is fresh coriander. Make sure there is no gravy. If the meat filling does not adhere, add a couple of boiled mashed potatoes to it, and mix it well, before stuffing the *samosas*.

18. Mix well by hand all the ingredients for the filling well by hand so that they stick together like a dough.

19. The most important thing to keep in mind is that the filling should be absolutely dry. The presence of any liquid makes it impossible to seal the *samosa*.

20. Make a little ball of the filling, and place it in the wrapper.

21. Fold, crimp, and fry as described above.

Makes 20

Zarina's Knockout Corn *Vade*

*D*eep fried corn savories

One 20-ounce packet of frozen corn, completely thawed in the packet
2 tablespoons chopped fresh ginger
4 cloves garlic
Salt to taste
2 teaspoons sugar
3 hot green peppers
½ teaspoon ground turmeric
½ teaspoon ground cayenne pepper
3 tablespoons all purpose flour
1 egg
3 tablespoons instant cream of wheat
2 cups oil for deep frying

1. Blend all the ingredients, *except* the oil, in an electric blender until a paste is made. This may take a while, but it will eventually be reduced to a paste in the blender! You may have to turn off the blender and mix the ingredients with a spatula, remove the spatula, cover the blender, and start the blending process again a couple of times, before you are successful.

2. Heat the oil in a wok on high heat, until a drop of the paste begins to sizzle, and fry briskly at once. Remove the drop of paste.

3. Drop the paste by the spoonful, 6 at a time, into the oil. The *vade* are done as soon as they turn reddish all over.

4. Remove the *vade* with a slotted spoon and place on 3 to 4 layers of paper towels for a minute or two.

5. Serve hot.

The corn *must* thaw completely before you blend it, or it does not make a paste.

Fantastically simple and simply fantastic!!

Serves 8

Fish Kababs

*F*ish cakes, made the Indian way!

2 pounds of any mild white fish fillet
4 cups water to boil the fish
2 large boiled potatoes, skins removed
2 eggs
1 tablespoon whole cumin seeds
1 tablespoon ground coriander seeds
1 teaspoon ground cayenne pepper
1 cup finely minced onion
1 tablespoon finely minced fresh ginger
Salt to taste
1 cup chopped fresh coriander
4 hot green peppers, finely minced
2 teaspoons *garam masala* (page 23)
1 cup oil to fry the fish cakes

1. Boil the fish, covered, in the water on medium high heat until done. This should take about 10 minutes.

2. Drain off the water, and allow the fish to cool.

3. When cool, mix the fish well with all other ingredients, *except* the oil.

4. Knead for a couple of minutes until soft, taking care that no chunks are left. Make fish cakes about 2 inches in diameter and ½ inch in thickness. Set aside on a tray. Heat oil in a non-stick frying pan on medium high heat. When the oil is ready, fry 4 to 5 cakes at a time. Turn over when one side is reddish brown. Then fry until the other side is reddish brown. The cakes should be fried crisp on both sides.

5. Place on 4 layers of paper towels for a few minutes before serving. The towels will soak up excess oil.

6. Serve hot, with ketchup or fresh chutney.

Makes about 25 kababs

Menus

The following pages list possible combinations for meals, from recipes in this book. These are only suggestions. You have to keep in mind that there should be

a) rice, and/or one of the breads and

b) a vegetarian or a non-vegetarian entree.

To make it a little elaborate, you could add

c) *dal* and

d) salad.

To make it a little more elaborate, also add

e) *raita* and

f) dessert.

If you want to serve a terribly sophisticated meal, add two or three entrees and/or a *pullao*.

It really is up to you. I have just combined items that I think would taste good together. You can delete or add items to make a menu that suits you better.

Rasam can be served as an appetizer before meals.

Samosas, Corn *Vade*, and Fish Kababs can be served with a Chutney, as snacks.

Vegetarian Meals

1. Plain Rice, Broccoli Rabe, Eggplant and Tomato Curry, Moong *Dal*, and *Khir*.
2. Plain Rice, *Dam Aloo, Dal*, Garlic Cabbage, and *Rasmalai*.
3. Plain Rice, Hot Broccoli, *Razmah*, Mint *Raita*, and *Bhappa Doi*.
4. Plain Rice, *Dal*, Broccoli Rabe, Fresh Chutney, and *Ghulab Jamun*.
5. Plain Rice, *Paneer Do Piaza, Dam Aloo, Cachumber Ka Salaad*, and *Kulfi*.
6. Vegetable *Pullao, Razmah*, Cucumber *Raita*, and *Kulfi*.
7. Vegetable *Pullao, Paneer Do Piaza, Bhindi Aloo, Beetroot Raita*, and *Ghulab Jamun*.
8. Vegetable *Pullao, Moti Mahal Dal*, Green Beans Curry, and Mango Soufflé.
9. *Chappati*, Cauliflower Curry, *Dal*, Orange Cucumber *Raita*, and *Ghulab Jamun*.
10. *Chappati*, Garlic Cabbage, Chick Peas, and *Khir*.
11. *Chappati, Bhindi Aloo*, Moong *Dal*, and *Khir*.
12. Plain *Paratha, Bhindi Aloo*, Cauliflower and Peas Curry, Mint *Raita*, and *Ghulab Jamun*.
13. Stuffed *Parathas*, Chick Peas, Hot Broccoli, Mint *Raita*, and *Khir*.
14. Stuffed *Paratha, Razmah, Cachumber Ka Salaad*, and *Ghulab Jamun*.
15. *Puri, Dosa Bhaji, Moti Mahal Dal, Cachumber Ka Salaad*, and *Khir*.
16. *Puri, Dosa Bhaji*, Chick Peas, *Cachumber Ka Salaad*, and *Rasmalai*.
17. A grand vegetarian meal would include Vegetable *Pullao, Puris*, Cauliflower and Peas, *Paneer Do Piaza, Bhindi Aloo, Moti Mahal Dal*, Everyday Salad, Mint *Raita*, and *Ghulab Jamun* or *Rasmalai*.

Non-Vegetarian Meals

1. Plain Rice, *Shami, Dam Aloo*, Hot Broccoli, and *Ghulab Jamun*.
2. Plain Rice, Chicken Curry, Green Beans, *Dal*, and *Bhappa Doi*.
3. Plain Rice, *Shami*, Hot Broccoli, Plain Yoghurt, and *Ghulab Jamun*.
4. Plain Rice, *Piaz* Chicken, *Dal*, Broccoli Rabe, and *Bhappa Doi*.
5. Plain Rice, *Sag Goshth*, Plain Yoghurt, Everyday Salad, and *Rasmalai*.
6. Plain Rice, *Kaliya*, Eggplant and Tomato Curry, *Razmah*, Orange Cucumber *Raita*, and *Ghulab Jamun*.
7. Plain Rice or Vegetable *Pullao, Roghanjosh*, Green Beans Curry, Mint Chutney, and *Ghulab Jamun*.
8. Plain Rice, *Awadhi Do Piaza, Bhindi Aloo, Dal*, Beetroot *Raita*, and *Ghulab Jamun*.
9. Plain Rice, Chutney Broiled Fish, Moong *Dal*, Garlic Cabbage, and *Bhappa Doi*.
10. Plain Rice, *Vindaloo, Dosa Bhaji*, Green Beans, and Mango Soufflé.
11. Plain Rice or Vegetable *Pullao, Machhere Jhol*, Moong *Dal*, Cauliflower and Peas Curry, *Cachumber Ka Salaad*, and *Bhappa Doi*.
12. Vegetable *Pullao*, Tikka Kabab, Garlic Cabbage, *Dal*, and Mango Soufflé.
13. Vegetable *Pullao, Bhuna* Lamb, *Khulla Keema*, Everyday Salad, and *Kulfi*.
14. Vegetable *Pullao*, Butter Chicken, *Cachumber Ka Salaad*, and *Kulfi*.
15. Vegetable *Pullao, Shahi Korma, Moti Mahal Dal, Cachumber Ka Salaad*, and *Kulfi*.
16. Vegetable *Pullao*, Tikka Kababs, *Razmah*, Orange Cucumber *Raita*, and *Kulfi*.
17. Lamb *Pullao, Dam Aloo, Razmah*, Mint *Raita*, and Mango Soufflé.
18. Lamb *Pullao, Yakhni, Razmah*, Broccoli Rabe, and *Kulfi*.
19. A grand dinner from Kashmir would include Lamb *Pullao, Roghanjosh, Kofte, Yakhni*, Broccoli Rabe *Haak, Razmah*, Walnut Mint Chutney, and *Rasmalai*.
20. Lamb *Pullao, Tandoori* Fish, Cauliflower and Peas Curry, and *Kulfi*.
21. Lamb *Biryani, Cachumber Ka Salaad*, Mint *Raita*, and *Kulfi*.
22. Lamb *Biryani, Shahi Korma*, Beetroot *Raita*, Everyday Salad, and *Ghulab Jamun*.
23. Lamb *Biryani, Piaz* Chicken, *Moti Mahal Dal, Bhindi Aloo*, Cucumber Orange *Raita*, and *Rasmalai*.
24. Lamb *Biryani, Tandoori* Chicken, Cauliflower and Peas Curry, *Cachumber Ka Salaad*, and *Rasmalai*.

25. *Khichdi*, *Dam Aloo*, Walnut Mint Chutney, and *Ghulab Jamun*.
26. Plain *Paratha*, *Kofte*, *Cachumber Ka Salaad*, and *Rasmalai*.
27. *Chappati*, Butter Chicken, *Moti Mahal Dal*, Everyday Salad, and *Kulfi*.

This is not an exhaustive list by any means.

Welcome to Indian Cuisine!

Index

Index